# LANGUAGE MATTERS

# LANGUAGE MATTERS

## Interviews with 22 Quebec Poets

edited by
Carolyn Marie Souaid
&
Endre Farkas

EDITIONS

Cover design by Doowah Design.
Interior design by Melody Morrissette.

This book was printed on Ancient Forest Friendly paper.
Printed and bound in Canada by Hignell Book Printing Inc.

We acknowledge the support of the Canada Council for the Arts and the Manitoba Arts Council for our publishing program.


*Library and Archives Canada Cataloguing in Publication*

Language matters (2013)
      Language matters : interviews with 22 Quebec poets / Carolyn Marie Souaid & Endre Farkas.

ISBN 978-1-927426-19-7 (pbk.)

1. Poets, Canadian (English)—Québec (Province)—20th century—Interviews. 2. Canadian poetry (English)—Québec (Province)—History and criticism. 3. Poetry—Authorship. 4. Poetics. 5. Poetry—Social aspects. 6. Poetry—Political aspects. I. Farkas, Endre, 1948-, interviewer (expression), editor of compilation II. Souaid, Carolyn Marie, 1959-, interviewer (expression), editor of compilation III. Title.

PS8295.5.Q8L35 2013      C811'.6099714      C2013-905428-6


·Signature Editions
P.O. Box 206, RPO Corydon, Winnipeg, Manitoba, R3M 3S7
www.signature-editions.com

# Contents

# Foreword

Look, he is
the nth Adam taking a green inventory
in world but scarcely uttered, naming, praising,
the flowering fiats in the meadow, the
syllabled fur, stars aspirate, the pollen
whose sweet collusion sounds eternally.

[ ... ]

And now in imagination he has climbed
another planet, the better to look
with single camera view upon this earth –
its total scope, and each afflated tick,
its talk, its trick, its tracklessness – and this,
           this he would like to write down in a book!

*– A.M. Klein, from "Portrait of the Poet as Landscape"*

God knows the creative process is a mystery. To make something out of nothing, to see a world in a blank page, to hear imagined people speak, to touch things that aren't there, to taste what is not yet baked, to speak volumes or write an image is something to wonder at, something awesome to behold. Yet these are the things that artists do every day. These are the tasks, pleasures and pains that artists, including poets, undertake. Transmitters of acts of the imagination, poets use language to make their unique works of art. But *how* do they do this?

This is one of the many questions we asked Quebec's English-language poets over the four-year lifespan of the online literary magazine that we, along with Elias Letelier, founded on June 24, 2009, Quebec's Fête Nationale. We were curious about their process but we also wondered whether living in Quebec and writing in the language of "les autres" meant anything aesthetically, socially, culturally and politically. We had a poetic and political agenda. *Poetry Quebec*, or *PQ*, was

POETRY PERSISTS BECAUSE IT IS LOW MAINTENANCE – ALL YOU NEED IS A REED PEN AND A CLAY TABLET, A BALLPOINT AND A SHEET OF PAPER.

**– CHARLOTTE HUSSEY**

a conscious and deliberate nod (and wink) to Quebec's separatist party, the Parti Québécois. We wanted through our tongue-in-cheek name and motto, "Je me souviens," to signal that Quebec's English-language poets are *Quebec poets* who were, are and will be here to remember and be remembered. The name and motto were also a manifesto of our engagement.

One thing that differentiates human beings from other creatures is consciousness. Through consciousness, humans are aware of their existence. Yes, philosophers, crackpots and artists may question the reality of this existence, but most seem to agree that humans are "aware" of the fact that they are aware. Just how aware is another question. But the degree of awareness is secondary to the fact that humans sit around fires, in caves, cafés, classrooms, and at desks long into the night, contemplating it.

Of course, this contemplation brings to light the big questions: Why and how did we come to be? We attempt to answer these and other questions through religion, science and the arts. Over the centuries, we have looked into the entrails of animals; we've looked to the heavens and explored the universe of our imagination. Our unquenchable need to know has led us to develop creative ways of looking and recording.

And for as long as we've had this awareness, we have had the arts. From the earliest cave paintings to the latest in body piercing and tattoos – all are evidence of our human attachment to the creative process.

Even those skeptical of the value of the arts – government leaders who favour no-nonsense pragmatism but who dole out obscene amounts of money for paintings of prime ministers and re-enactments of the "great" battles of yesteryear, or big business entrepreneurs who focus on the bottom line but spend billions developing the perfect shade of lipstick – do not deny that the arts exist. In evolutionary terms, with respect to human beings, we could call the arts a necessary appendage or scheme, since Darwinian theory posits that all appendages and schemes adopted by creatures are geared toward the survival of the species. The creative process by which we make art is therefore an essential aspect of human existence and survival, and a subject worth investigating.

Right from its inaugural issue, *Poetry Quebec* was interested in the creative process of Quebec's English-language poets and how it related to their engagement with private, public, local and global concerns, issues and themes. As editors, we felt that aiming a spotlight on this process through interviews as well as essays, articles, and reviews of their books was important not only for the poets but for

A POET IS A MINORITY WHEREVER SHE IS.

**– GILLIAN SZE**

the English- and French-language communities of Quebec. The interviews would allow readers to learn more about the poets but also something about themselves and their relationship to language and the creative process. And here in Quebec – especially – being aware of language is vital. It matters.

Although the first poem written in Canada in one of the colonizing languages, "The Pleasant Life in Newfoundland," is claimed by Robert Hayman in 1628, in Newfoundland, scholars agree that real poetic activity in Canada began in Quebec, specifically in Montreal in the early 1800s, with Levi Adams.

"A Canadian," according to the scholar Arthur L. Phelps, "is one who is increasingly aware of being an American in the continental sense without being American in the national sense" (*Literary History of Canada, Volume One,* 139). And this sense of being a Canadian – English – began in Lower Canada with Adams. His social observations, his description of French Canadians, places him in a tradition continued through A.M. Klein. Adams's book-length poem "Jean Baptiste" was published in Montreal in 1825: "The place of publication is worth noting ... since a Canadian imprint was rare," notes Phelps (*LHC,* 141-2). His poem was warmly reviewed in *Canadian Review* and *Canadian Magazine,* both Montreal-based literary magazines. Poetic activity was beginning to surface with this and subsequent publications such as *The Quebec Gazette* (Quebec City) and Montreal's *Literary Garland,* which also ran poems and reviews.

The first wave of Modernism in poetry in Canada also began in Montreal with the publication of the first issue of *The McGill Fortnightly Review* on November 21, 1925. Two of the prime movers behind its founding and editing were A.J.M. Smith and F.R. Scott, two graduate students attending McGill University (Ken Norris, *The Little Magazine in Canada 1925–80*). Another important member of this Montreal group to emerge was A.M. Klein, probably the most urban and cosmopolitan of them. As the "theoretician" among them, Smith defined, most clearly, his view of the purpose and quality of the modern in his article "Contemporary Poetry":

Our age is an age of change, and of a change that is taking place with a rapidity unknown in any other epoch.... Our universe is a different one from that of our grandfathers, nor can our religious beliefs be the same. The whole movement, indeed, is a movement away from an erroneous but comfortable stability, towards a more truthful and sincere but certainly less comfortable state of flux. Ideas are changing, and therefore manners

9

and morals are changing. It is not surprising, then, to find that the arts, which are an intensification of life and thought, are likewise in a state of flux. (in Norris, 14)

Although this does not directly address the poet's creative process, it is a manifesto of the poetics and aesthetics with which he, Scott and Klein were engaged. Through poetry, they were exploring and forging what James Joyce called "the uncreated conscience" of his race.

Quebec was also the birthplace for the second wave of Modernism in poetry and literature in Canada. This post-World War II movement was led by Louis Dudek and Irving Layton. Dudek was its thinker and Layton its high priest. While Dudek was interested in writing poetically and polemically about the struggle to make poetry matter, Layton shouted and sang about the poetic and prophetic role of the poet. Layton was probably the first Canadian poet to make the poet and the creative process the theme and topic of his poems. Not only did he introduce Canadians to sex, as he claims, he held strong opinions on just about every topic under the sun – and moon. Layton gave us a sense that every poet must be "engaged." Through the poetry of Dudek, Layton and later Leonard Cohen, Canadians were exposed to the idea that the private and public lives of poets mattered to the local and global consciousness of the individual and the collective.

The 1970s saw the rise of turbulent political times in Quebec. Francophone aspirations for independence were stirring. A number of those leading the way were artists, including the poets Gérald Godin and Gaston Miron. Meanwhile, English-language poets, on the whole, were silent on this issue. Most were apolitical or sympathetic "outsiders." Their sense of isolation grew as the English-language poetic focus shifted from Quebec to Ontario, and to Toronto in particular.

In spite of this shift, or perhaps because of it, a group of poets, dubbed the Vehicule Poets – Endre Farkas, Artie Gold, Tom Konyves, Claudia Lapp, John McAuley, Stephen Morrissey and Ken Norris – emerged. The seven worked individually and collectively to revive the dormant English-language poetry scene in Quebec, the reality of which included being a "minority within a minority":

English poetry in Montreal has always been written under the most unique conditions. Being a member of a minority culture within the bounds of a dominant francophone community has made the English poet in Montreal intensely aware of his own language as well as informing him of the problem inherent in the use of language as an agent of communication. When he writes, the Montreal poet knows that the vast majority of people living in his city have no interest whatsoever in what he has to say because what he is saying is in a language that has no relevance to their cultural life. He also recognizes that because he is Québécois, he is isolated from English Canada. The third disadvantage he experiences is that the isolated anglophone community, unlike the francophone, does not consider its arts as necessary for survival; rather, the modus operandi has been economic dominance. (*Montreal English Poetry of the Seventies*, Farkas and Norris, ix)

The contextualizing introduction of *Montreal English Poetry of the Seventies* and the sheer volume of contributors to the book, twenty-two in all, staked out a claim for the existence of Quebec's English-language poets. The variety and quality of the poetry attested to their diversity and vitality. During this period, the Vehicule Poets themselves conducted an exploration into their own creative processes in a "round table" discussion with Louis Dudek, published in 1979 by Maker Press, entitled *A Good Goosing*.

From the mid-1980s to the mid-1990s, the Quebec English-language literary community went missing, or into hibernation. The reasons were many. It's not that there weren't any poets around, or that they weren't writing. Whatever was going on just wasn't very public. This invisibility started to change when two Montreal writers, Ray Beauchemin and Denise Roig, launched The Urban Wanderers Reading Series, which played a pivotal role in helping to resuscitate and revitalize Montreal's once-vibrant English-language literary tradition. Born out of "a hunger to hear the voices among us," according to one of its co-producers, the series began in the fall of 1993 and ran successfully for three seasons in a trendy bistro on the Main. The Monday night series featured English writers in Montreal "exploring the twin landscapes of poetry and prose." More precisely, they were "...Urban – born in Montreal, or borne to Montreal in the cars of rented Ryder trucks" and they were "Wanderers – dissecting the roots of what we call home, roots of the languages we speak; unsure of what comes next but not always comfortable with what we find now." (*The Urban Wanderers Reader*, 1995, vii)

Flash forward to the "new" millennium, and to *PQ*, launched to celebrate and remember the significant and innovative contributions of Quebec's English-language poets, past and present. Our main objective was to harness the power of the Internet to offer English-language poets a more visible platform. One of the

WE HAVE THE POWER TO CHANGE PEOPLE'S MINDS, TO AFFECT THEM IN GREATER WAYS THAN A POLITICAL SPEECH OR A COMMERCIAL COULD, BY ACTIVATING THE SOUL'S VOICE.

– MOE CLARK

ways we did this was by publishing online interviews with poets to provide insight into their creative process and to share with readers the extent to which living in Quebec affected their aesthetics, writing and consciousness. While the present volume is only a sampling of the many interviews published during our nearly four years of existence, it is nevertheless a veritable cross-section of the Who's Who of Quebec's thriving poetry scene. Among the criteria for inclusion was choosing those who had the most interesting and insightful things to say about living and working in this politically charged and often volatile province.

Is writing in English in Quebec a political act? The responses we got ranged from one end of the spectrum to the other. David McGimpsey argues it's hardly a threat to one's personal liberty: "It may not get you many friends at a Loco Lacasse concert but nobody is going to put you in jail because you wrote a poem called 'Camille Laurin Stinks!'" Others, like Jason Camlot, believe the context of production and reception are important considerations: "... when Michèle Lalonde used English in her poem 'Speak White' and read it before an audience of thousands at the first Nuit de la poésie in Montreal in 1970, she was engaged in a politically-motivated language act, and... the use of English in her poem was received as a political act by her audience." Erín Moure, for whom "writing in English, picking up a pen and writing, is not necessarily a 'political' act," weighs in on the issue from her perspective as someone raised in English in Alberta, but whose expansive playing field is language itself: "The act of writing in English and including French directly in the poem is a political act, though. The act of writing and speaking in Galician is a political act."

As a document that will be of interest to scholars as well as those of the general public with more than a passing interest in poetry, *Language Matters* includes a small sampling from each poet, and, in some cases, a window into their creative process. The contributors range in age across four decades. They are unilingual, bilingual, multilingual. They are multicultural and gender-diverse. They include traditional, page-based poets, as well as LANGUAGE-influenced and performance-oriented poets. They are native Quebecers and *nouveaux-arrivés* from the rest of Canada and elsewhere in the world. They speak white, black, and every colour in between.

Mainly, they speak poetry.

Carolyn Marie Souaid
Endre Farkas
*Montreal, 2013*

IF I HAVE A FAVOURITE IT IS EVERYBODY'S FAVOURITE: LEONARD COHEN.

**— MARY DI MICHELE**

# Stephanie Bolster

Stephanie Bolster's latest book, *A Page from the Wonders of Life on Earth*, was shortlisted for the Pat Lowther Award, and an excerpt from her new project was chosen as a finalist for the CBC/Canada Writes competition in 2012. Her first book, *White Stone: The Alice Poems*, won the Governor General's Award and the Gerald Lampert Award in 1998. Her work has also received the Bronwen Wallace Award, the Archibald Lampman Award, and *The Malahat Review*'s long poem prize, among other awards, and has been translated into French, Spanish, and German. She edited *The Best Canadian Poetry in English 2008* and *The Ishtar Gate: Last and Selected Poems* by the Ottawa poet Diana Brebner, and co-edited *Penned: Zoo Poems*. Born in Vancouver, she teaches creative writing at Concordia University and lives in Pointe-Claire, Quebec.

***Poetry Quebec:* Where are you originally from and how did you end up in Quebec?**
*Stephanie Bolster:* I was born in Vancouver, grew up in Burnaby, BC, and moved to Montreal in 2000 when I was hired by Concordia's Department of English.

**When did you first become interested in poetry?**
Like many kids, I remember writing haiku in grade two; unlike most, I enjoyed the experience. As a child, I wanted to write children's books and most of what I read was prose. It was only when I was fifteen or sixteen that poetry emerged as a serious focus for me.

**What triggered the shift?**

Like many teens, I was self-absorbed, and poetry – or, at least, most lyric poetry – permits Romantic self-expression more readily than does prose fiction. When I was sixteen, a friend shared some Sylvia Plath poems with me, and their intensity and impeccable craft made me fall in love with poetry even more fully as both a reader and a writer.

**How did you encounter your first Quebec poem?**
I don't tend to think in terms of the provincial origins of poems and especially didn't do so when I first began reading poetry. I suspect, though, that my first Quebec poem would have been one by Leonard Cohen, read in an introduc-

tory Canadian Literature course as an undergrad at the University of British Columbia.

## What is your working definition of a poem?

I don't really have one, though as a teacher I like to begin my classes with the question of defining poetry, because it reveals a lot about the students' preconceptions. I'm more interested in pushing beyond implicit boundaries than in defining them. Increasingly, I'm drawn to work that disregards genre.

## Whose work does this for you, and how does it do so?

W.G. Sebald is the writer whose work I'd most like to have written. Although his best known work is in prose, most of it is not fiction (or, at least, not obviously so), and his "novel," *Austerlitz*, is written in an unparagraphed, meandering prose that bears more resemblance to the essay than to most novels. And yet, in spirit, all his work feels more akin to poetry than to prose. By this I mean, in part, that it is associative rather than narrative, and that it privileges intuition – but even to express the distinctions in these terms is to generalize about genres in ways that I resist.

The poet Robert Hass has been a significant influence on me, and his poems are, increasingly, extended meditations that resemble essays and are often written in very long lines with few stanza breaks. Anne Carson's work, too, plays with other modes and structures. And then there are exciting Canadian (indeed, Montreal) writers like Sina Queyras and Erín Moure, whose work, though much more obviously poetry than any other genre, draws upon found

material and translation, among other sources/practices.

All of these writers seem more interested in the integrity of the work that they are producing than in how it will be labeled after the fact. It is that sense of originality and authenticity that I admire and seek to achieve.

## Fairly early in your career, you won the Governor General's Award for *White Stone: The Alice Poems*. How did this affect or change your writing life?

I felt, and still feel, enormously fortunate to have won the GG, particularly at that time in my life. (I won't say "career," because before receiving the award, I didn't think of myself as having a career.) Prizes are far less random than lotteries, but, nevertheless, they involve a strong element of chance. Because that particular jury in that particular year selected my book, I achieved a public recognition that I might not have achieved otherwise. National interviews on CBC radio, a profile in *The Ottawa Citizen*, an invitation to read to 200 people at a lunchtime event at the National Arts Centre, these were a few of the immediate benefits. I was invited to give readings and workshops whereas, prior to the award, I had to seek out such opportunities myself.

I was also fortunate that my second book, *Two Bowls of Milk*, had already been accepted by McClelland & Stewart; I was in the process of completing the final revisions when I received the news about the GG. So there was no immediate pressure to produce another book, and I already knew that the work I was writing, which eventually became *Pavilion*, didn't resemble *White Stone* to a great extent. If people wanted me to

STEPHANIE BOLSTER

write that book again – and many still do – they would just have to be disappointed. I'd already moved on.

I think, too, that having that good fortune so early in my career freed me from worrying about prizes. The chances of lucking out again seemed slim, and the door that a prize can open had already opened for me at a crucial time. So, if anything, that award gave me the confidence to rely on my own standards and instincts rather than trying to second-guess what juries or readers might think.

**Do you have a writing ritual?**

I try to write early in the day, before e-mail and the To Do list take over, but in practice, it's hard to stick to those rules. I write on the computer – anything written on paper feels provisional for me – and need to feel myself alone to write well, even if there are other people around. I don't listen to music, though I do usually have a bunch of books lying around – reference books pertaining to what I'm writing about, art books, books of poetry – and increasingly Googling comes into my writing process. This lets the poems be more digressive and fact-rich, though it also wastes a lot of time.

**You say that the newer technologies have contributed to a change in the way you approach the writing of a poem. Have they directly impacted on the final poems themselves?**

Because my computer is the site of both research and writing, I often find myself cutting and pasting material from websites into my working documents. Often, that text remains source material that I mine for details, but sometimes it shows up in the poem as found text. My work has always drawn upon research, and my two most recent books have included a lot of quoted text. But doing research online has heightened my awareness of borrowing – because I'm not even pretending to make the words my own by typing them up from a book, but, rather, dropping them into my poem – and also made me more interested in charting the process and interaction of research and composition.

A line from my long poem-in-progress, in a passage referring to my late maternal grandmother, reads, "Someone on Facebook has her name." Other passages, as yet unpublished and difficult to excerpt, refer to virtual visits to sites by way of Google Street View. And in a poem from my most recent book, "A Brief History of the Bear Pit in the Ménagerie du Jardin des Plantes," a webcam makes an appearance.

I'm still figuring out how process-oriented the poems can be without being self-indulgent, sloppy, or simply dull. I'm also aware of the fact that those who are really into technology and social media have found Facebook, Google, and YouTube passé for some time now, so I need to be aware of the impact that such references will have on the work by the time it appears in book form.

**What is your approach to writing a poem?**

Once I find a subject, a concept, I tend to write around it for quite a long time – i.e., a long poem, a series of poems, or a whole manuscript – and having an ongoing subject helps me to sit down to write even if I'm not feeling inspired. That said, occasional poems do simply arise sometimes and I try to make way

STEPHANIE BOLSTER

for them even if I should be doing something else.

## How does parenthood inspire and/or interfere with your poetry?

The inspiration is boundless – I have calendars full of astonishing things my daughters have said and done. The freshness that they bring to observation and the imagination that they bring to life cannot be anything other than inspiring. But of course the time I spend doing things with and for them is time that I might otherwise have spent writing. I once heard a writer say, "Every child is a lost novel." I don't find it useful to think in those terms. I'm an utterly different person because of being a parent, which means that I'm an utterly different poet. My children don't show up in my poems very often, but the fact that they are in my life lies behind everything I write. I'll most likely produce fewer books during the next couple of decades than would have been the case otherwise, but those books will, I believe, be richer than they would have been. Or maybe not even richer; maybe just different.

## Does being part of the English-speaking minority in Quebec impact on your writing?

As a poet, I'm used to being on the margins, so living in Quebec grants a kind of anonymity that can be conducive to writing. I also appreciate the ways in which understanding French expands my understanding of the world – when I've been speaking or listening to French a great deal, I think differently – and also the ways in which my lack of complete fluency enables me to turn off francophone conversations in public places, allowing me to be alone with my thoughts while in a crowd, hearing tantalizing tidbits but not being tempted to eavesdrop.

## Would you say that writing in English in Quebec is a political act?

No. Perhaps I'd feel differently if I'd grown up here, but because there is a large anglophone readership in Canada outside of Quebec, and a readership – limited but healthy – here, I don't feel I'm going out on a limb by writing in English. For me to write in French would be a political act.

## Why do you write?

It's how I think, how I feel, how I understand the world.

## Who is your audience?

Myself, first of all. After that, like-minded people. And, ranging farther, unlike-minded people who might, through reading my work, come to a new understanding of the world and/or themselves.

## Do you think there is an audience, outside of friends or other poets, for poetry?

Of course. It's a small one, but it's there, and in some countries it's quite significant. I've met people who are devout poetry readers but don't write.

## On the other hand, here, in Canada, aside from needing a good quote for a funeral or a wedding toast, adults rarely crack open a book of poetry once they've left school. What responsibility do teachers have in fostering readers of poetry?

By the time students enter my classes at Concordia, they've pretty much already made a decision that poetry matters to them – or, at least, that literature matters. (Undergrads in our creative writing program are required to write in at least two genres, so some of my students are fiction writers who are afraid of playwriting.) But those students are a very select group.

Before I was hired at Concordia I often gave writing workshops in schools, and I came to realize that there was a great potential to engage students in poetry in elementary school, and that by the time students had reached even the upper grades of elementary school, the window of opportunity for deep poetic engagement seemed to have closed. Often, the classroom teachers were relieved when I showed up because they felt ill at ease discussing poetry with the students, even though the class in question might be a grade two class. How much expertise does one need to get a group of seven-year-olds expressing themselves? It seemed to me that, even at an early stage, teachers felt the need to instill in students an analytical, as opposed to an expressive and observational, intent. Kids who enjoy writing poetry will enjoy reading it and vice versa. Attention to the five senses, to comparisons, to the music of language, goes a long way. Teachers can have a huge impact at that stage. But because most of today's teachers grew up with little poetry exposure themselves – and much of that probably unsatisfying – they don't have a sense of how rich and varied poetry can be, nor of the fact that it needn't be "decoded" in order to be appreciated.

## Do you feel that high school English teachers are equipped to effectively teach poetry to their students?

Because they are specialized in particular subject areas as elementary teachers aren't, high school English teachers are far less likely to have the same poetry phobias, but they are even more guilty of instilling an analytical approach in their students. This is a gross generalization, I realize; there are wonderful teachers out there who love poetry and share that love with their students. But many get bogged down in scansion and symbol. And, to be honest, I'm not sure that poetry is even taught much in high school English classes. I tend to get e-mails from high school students during April when they're working on essays or presentations on my poems, and it seems pretty clear that most teachers relegate poetry to a "unit" during National Poetry Month and forget about it the rest of the time.

## Does your day job as a professor impact on your writing?

On a practical level, having a day job takes time, which means that there's less time to write. But I'm fortunate enough to have a day job that lets me think about writing, specifically about poetry, much of the time. Teaching makes me a better reader of poetry; it hones my editorial sense, makes me less willing to accept – as a writer and as a reader – easy or rote formulations. Ultimately, that makes me a better writer, too, though because it makes me tougher on myself, it can feel like an obstacle at times.

## How hard is it to switch hats from being the critical editor to the poet once you leave the classroom? In other words, how do you leave the work at work?

Good question! I'm still trying to figure that out. The short answer is: I don't. And, since having children, I've found it impossible to get any significant amount of writing done during the academic year. Sometimes, there is simply so

STEPHANIE BOLSTER

much work to be done that the poet in me doesn't even have enough space to notice things and offer lines here and there. But during the spring and summer, I can work on a poem of my own in the morning and critique poems by a thesis student during the afternoon and not feel any conflict. The trick is to do my own work first. Otherwise I'm finished. And during the academic year, I simply can't do my own work first or the students won't get their due.

**So, then, finding time is the toughest part of writing for you?**

At this point, yes. It's hard to make peace with myself, with the fact that writing is essential but that other things also need to be done. Finding a balance is difficult. If I try to clear the decks (like answering these interview questions!) before I begin writing, I'll never begin writing; there's always something To Do. On the other hand, if I cloister myself, things that need to get done don't get done, people around me get frustrated, and I cheat myself out of the life experiences that make me a richer person, which in turn make me a richer poet.

**What are you working on now?**

For several years, I've been working on what I think will be a book-length poem which takes as its point of departure various series of post-disaster photographs – of such sites as post-Katrina New Orleans and Pripyat (Chernobyl) – by the Montreal-born photographer Robert Polidori. Like many long poems, it's a pretty digressive entity, and I'm still figuring out what its boundaries might be. The poem interrogates, among other things, the act and responsibility of witnessing and of artistic transformation.

I need to have a concept before I begin to think of poems as a book. That concept is rarely clear at the outset, but without it, I do feel as if I'm spinning my wheels. A poem that doesn't tie in to anything else, though it may be published in a journal, doesn't feel quite worthy for me. I'm at my best when working in longer poems or series.

**How many drafts do you usually go through before you are satisfied with a poem?**

This varies enormously. Some poems (though a very few) remain relatively unchanged from their initial drafts. Most, though, go through ... five? ten? fifteen drafts? What is a draft? I think of the process more in terms of time, and many of my poems take several years before they find their "final" form, by which I mean the form on which I settle, before moving on.

[In class] I give my students a handout that presents four drafts of one of my early *Alice* poems as a means of illustrating the kinds of changes one can make. These days, I'm more likely to rewrite a poem/section from scratch than to tinker with it as I did back then, but these drafts illustrate the fact that my revision process did and does consist largely of removing what seems extraneous. I refer to this handout as "the incredible shrinking poem."

**What is your idea of a muse?**

A photograph, a painting, a line of poetry or music, a scene, a fascinating fact, that makes me turn to the keyboard or pull out paper and a pen.

**Do you have a favourite time and place to write?**

At the beginning or at the end of the day, in my office at home, beside the window.

STEPHANIE BOLSTER

### Is travel important to your writing practice?

I love to travel. It unsettles me, and this ultimately makes for good writing. I have to be wary, though, of relying upon the exoticism of travel or the gap between expectation and reality, about which I tend to write frequently. I rarely write much while travelling; it's often not until years after a trip that it will manifest itself in poems.

### Do you write about Quebec?

Not consciously; to do so would mean being more socially motivated than I am as a writer at this point. I'm more interested in psychology and aesthetics than in politics or sociology. I've written about the paintings of Jean-Paul Lemieux and about my move here from BC, but now that this place is home, I'm less aware of it, and when I am, that awareness hasn't, so far, translated into poems. I'm more interested in Montreal as a city than I am in Quebec as a province. I'd like to write more about the roughness of the city; the fact that the city is not as constantly and consciously remaking itself as Vancouver and Toronto are comforts and inspires me, because it implies a respect for history and leaves space for individual identities to assert themselves. ∎

STEPHANIE BOLSTER

*Two Drafts*

## 25 April 1856

How was it that first time, did they meet
through a simple raising of eyebrows, curious:
her about these 2 tall men with cumbersome
paraphernalia, him about these 3 little girls
playing in the Deanery garden.

The men had come to photograph the Cathedral,
but Dodgson put the children
in the foreground, an experiment:
first the flood of chemicals, *collodion* and *silver nitrate*,
then 45 long seconds of stillness,
and she only 4 and quick.

He was 24 then, did not choose her
as his favourite until the *Adventures*
6 years later. But something began
that afternoon, marked in his diary with a white stone.

Perhaps it was the garden, Alice and her sisters
2 years on either side of her, blooming amongst
the flowers of April, in England.
Her hair a brown thatch, cut straight
across the forehead, her dark blue eyes
tight buds. The possibilities of spring
and he only 24 and searching.

Although accustomed to gazes, to arranging
hands (her father was Dean of Christ Church, her mother
dressed the girls the same, so they would look
a picture) Alice remembered this one man, remembered
his stiffness, as though he had swallowed a poker.
He seemed afraid of her, and that was something,

her only 4 and him old enough
to be her father, how they both stood
tense and ticking
in the infinite unfurling garden
during the long exposure.

STEPHANIE BOLSTER

## Aperture, 1856

First the flood of chemicals:
guncotton, ether, silver
nitrate. Then forty-five long seconds
of stillness – and she only three
and quick. Did they meet because

of a raising of eyebrows, curiouser
about each other than about anyone
else in the garden? Her sisters
blurred into foliage;
he smelled of medicine. He was

twenty-four, did not choose her
as his favourite until the *Adventures*
six years later. But something began
that afternoon, marked in his diary
"with a white stone."

Her blue eyes tight buds.
Her mousy thatch straight across
the forehead. Spring everywhere threatening
to open them both: tense in that unfurling
garden, during the long exposure.

STEPHANIE BOLSTER

After his first meeting with Alice Liddell on 25 April, 1856, Charles Dodgson wrote in his diary, "I mark this day with a white stone." The expression originates in Catullus' "*Lapide candidiore diem notare*," (Poem 68, line 148) which translates as "to mark with an especially white stone the (lucky) day." The English version was quite commonly used in Victorian times.

# Mark Abley

Photo: John Mahoney

MARK ABLEY

Mark Abley has written three books of poetry: *Blue Sand, Blue Moon* (Cormorant, 1988), *Glasburyon* (Quarry, 1994) and *The Silver Palace Restaurant* (McGill-Queen's, 2005). "Glasburyon," a poetic elegy for dying languages, has been translated into Esperanto and Jèrriais. At the moment he is preparing a volume of new and selected poems.

He has also written two children's books and five books of non-fiction. The most recent, *Conversations With a Dead Man: The Legacy of Duncan Campbell Scott*, was submitted on deadline to Douglas & McIntyre Ltd. in October 2012, the same week that the publisher entered bankruptcy protection. Such episodes of bad luck, even though they hurt, don't begin to match all the good luck he received in winning a Rhodes Scholarship and a Guggenheim Fellowship, marrying an amazing woman and fathering two tremendous daughters.

### *Poetry Quebec:* Are you a native Quebecer?

*Mark Abley:* I'm not a native Quebecer but it's hard to say where I'm from – by the time I was twelve, I had lived in England, northern Ontario, England again, Alberta, and finally Saskatchewan. If pressed, I usually say I'm from Saskatoon. In 1983, I came to Montreal – not quite the same thing, emotionally, as coming to Quebec – at the age of twenty-eight. My wife and I were moving to Canada from a bucolic English village, and we wanted to see if a large bilingual city could be our home.

### What made you stay?

Friendship was a big part of the reason. From the start, we made good friends here. I'd sometimes been lonely as a boy, but I don't recall ever feeling lonely in those early years in Montreal. We adopted a couple of wonderful kittens too. Besides which, we had the pleasure of discovering the diverse neighbourhoods and landscapes and histories of Montreal.

In 1986, and again in 1987, I spent a few months living in Toronto, working as an editor for *Saturday Night* magazine. I was offered a permanent job as a result. But by then my sense of home was intimately tied to my sense of Montreal.

## When did you encounter your first Quebec poem?

Listening to *Songs of Leonard Cohen* on the stereo player in my family's living room when I was in high school. That means I encountered ten of them at once. I still know a few by heart. "When my life was a leaf that the seasons tore off and condemned, the songs bound me with love that was graceful and green as a stem."

## How did you first become interested in poetry?

I was fourteen when I realized that I wanted to be a writer – not necessarily, or not just, a poet. A little later I bought *A Pocket Book of Modern Verse*, edited by Oscar Williams. I can still recall sitting in a grassy park on a warm day in Saskatoon, my mind lit up by the discoveries. By the time I was sixteen, I was convinced that I absolutely had to be a poet.

## At sixteen, what did "being a poet" mean to you?

The power to rise above what was thwarting me or scaring me, and to create a work of art of my own. My father was a church organist, choirmaster and music teacher, and he would often compose music too – I think he was happiest when he could wander around the house with a pencil behind his ear and scribble down musical notes and phrases on the back of an old envelope. Or even put down his fork, grab his pencil, and do this at the dinner table. Yet he was also depressed about what he saw as his failure – the jobs he had and the money he earned were never commensurate with the tremendous musi-

cal talent he'd shown in boyhood. So I grew up with an intimate sense of both the difficulties and the rewards of art. I wasn't particularly musical, I couldn't draw, I couldn't dance, I was too shy to act – words were the only thing left. But I always felt, to misquote Samuel Beckett, that even if I didn't have anything much to express, I had an obligation to express. And when I felt frustrated, as teenagers inevitably do, I discovered that writing poems could offer a therapeutic release – not that I would have wanted to use such a phrase back then.

I was lucky, too. At the age of sixteen, before I was sure I had a real talent for writing, I was asked to join a poetry workshop that took place every couple of weeks in different homes across Saskatoon. The informal leader of the group was a wonderful poet, Anne Szumigalski. I imagine she looked on me as a kind of protégé and I certainly saw her as a mentor. Joining that group, having my poems read and taken seriously by some very smart and honest people, was the best affirmation an aspiring poet could ever have.

## Are these the same motivations that drive you today?

I don't think I need the therapeutic release and I certainly don't need the social affirmation. In fact I've begun to shy away from the literary scene. My career as a journalist, the column on language I still write for *The Gazette*, the non-fiction books I've published – all this means I no longer get any particular thrill out of seeing my name in print. But I still feel an underlying need to write poems. As a boy I was very religious, and the feeling that somehow I have to justify myself before God is something that runs very deep, even today when the traditional sense of God no longer satisfies my thinking self. My unthinking self goes on feeling that I must have something to offer, something beautiful, something meaningful, to justify my time on Earth.

## What is your working definition of a poem?

Why do we need a definition? I try to avoid it. Definitions fix ideas in amber, whereas poems wriggle free. Or to turn theological again, I don't think a strict definition of God helps anyone to be more religious or to understand the universe better; it just ties God up in conceptual knots. The same goes for poetry.

## How do you approach the writing of a poem?

Nothing works for me without an initial inspiration, and inspiration can't be forced. After that shard or scrap of inspiration – an image, a phrase, a memory, a place, whatever – then the hard work begins. I tend to rewrite a lot. I wish I'd rewritten some of my early poems a lot more. When I was younger, I was satisfied too easily.

Here's an example: Thirty years ago, when like many people I was worried about the threat of nuclear annihilation, I wrote a poem based on Jan Vermeer's painting "A View of Delft." I learned that Vermeer had painted this marvelously serene cityscape only a few years after a terrible explosion and fire had ripped through Delft – a gunpowder store exploded, killing more than a hundred people. So the painting became a kind of allegory, if you like, for the violence that can lie below a graceful surface. I imagined that when the explosion occurred, Vermeer had been holding a Spanish painting: "two remorseful saints / and a sombre Christ who fell from his arms ..." The whole mood of the poem, not just the Spanish painting, is sombre, so I didn't need that adjective – much later, I changed it to "stubbled." I also noticed that most of the sentences ended at a line-break, making the rhythm somewhat monotonous, so now I've altered a few of those line-breaks. And two lines used to read: "perhaps a function of the recent war / or the prospect of the one to come." How could I have put three "the's" in a row like that? Now I've made it "a prospect," and the line reads much better. All these changes are small, I realize, and they may sound almost insignificant. But together, I think they make the poem sharper and better.

## How many drafts do you usually go through before you are finished, or at least satisfied, with a poem?

It varies. Now it often takes me eight or ten drafts – or more. The form and shape of a poem usually come clear at an early stage. I never begin with a sonnet, let's say, and later turn it into a ballad. But if a sonnet is what I'm writing – and this doesn't happen often, though I have written a few – I will tinker relentlessly with the images, the rhythms, the rhymes, the verb tenses and so on. After a while I'll get to a point where I'm momentarily satisfied, and then I'll press "Save." But when I come back and look at the poem an hour or a day later, I almost invariably find something else to change.

Part of the trick, of course, is knowing when to stop tinkering. It's possible to over-revise, over-intellectualize, over-interpret, and then a poem can lose the freshness and spontaneity that gave it life in the first place.

**Are there central themes that you keep coming back to in your poetry or is each book a new adventure?**

Loss. That's what inspires me most – the threat of loss, the fact of loss, or the aftermath of loss. I don't mean that I ever wake up and think, "Today I'm going to write another poem about loss." But if I were an academic, God forbid, writing an analysis of my own poetry, loss is where I would begin. If it were a lengthy analysis, I'd move on from loss to time – though perhaps that's another way of saying the same thing.

**Does being part of the English-speaking minority in Quebec influence or affect your writing?**

I'm sure it does, but not always in obvious ways. Our minority status tends to make us more aware of the arbitrary quality inherent in any language and also of the incongruities that emerge when languages mingle and clash. I suspect the battle to keep French vibrant in Quebec – even when I find it tiresome and tiring – has been a kind of inspiration for me. My book *Spoken Here: Travels Among Threatened Languages* said little about Quebec directly. Yet indirectly, Quebec's influence was enormous.

Living here, it's very difficult for anyone to take language for granted. Issues involving language in this province have a seriousness that people in places like Wales or Catalonia instinctively grasp. In the rest of Canada, and much of the United States, people often don't get it. We baffle them – and by "we," I mean both English- and French-speaking Quebecers.

**Do you think that English, despite being the language of the North American majority, is under threat in Quebec?**

No! Absolutely not. I realize that I might feel differently if I'd grown up in the Gaspé or the Lower North Shore or even perhaps the Eastern Townships. But here in Montreal, it would be a mistake to confuse legitimate annoyances with actual threats. It's annoying if a bus-driver can't or won't address a passenger in English. It's annoying if a store clerk or a waitress refuses to switch to English even when a customer has little or no French. But English continues to be spoken regularly by a million or so people in Montreal, almost all of whom have access to mass media of every kind in the English language. That's a far cry from threat.

Let me tell you what threat is. I've written about it in many articles as well as in *Spoken Here*. Threat is what faces the remaining speakers of French in Alberta or Newfoundland or Saskatchewan, who can't pay their heating bills or phone bills in their own language, can't get medical or legal services in their own language, don't have any local magazines or newspapers in their own language, and so on. None of that applies to English in Montreal. Here in Quebec, "threat" is what's facing the speakers of Innu and Mohawk, Mi'kmaq and Cree, Inuktitut and Algonquin. Years ago, in a little town near Sorel, I met an old woman, Cécile Wawanolett, who was one of the last few fluent speakers of the Abenaki language. She's dead now, and while Abenaki will probably survive to a small extent as a ceremonial language, it may be effectively extinct as a fully living tongue.

MARK ABLEY

**For you, is writing in English in Quebec a political act?**

Not particularly. I would agree that to write in English in Quebec is to perform an act of witness, but I wouldn't go beyond that. In our society, poetry has a very small public role, and poets who claim otherwise are probably engaged in wishful thinking.

**Why do you write?**

Because I have to.

**Do you sense that people have a fear of poetry or is it general apathy?**

I suspect the two are related, although I'd prefer the word "intimidated" rather than "fearful." A lot of people expect poetry to be difficult; they expect it will make them feel stupid because they don't understand it or enjoy it. They're not necessarily hostile to it, or even scared of it, but they feel intimidated by it. I imagine composers of serious contemporary music face the same issue. Because the potential audience doesn't believe in the possibility of gaining pleasure from the experience, they deny themselves the experience. And so they become apathetic.

**Do you think there is an audience, outside of friends or other poets, for poetry?**

Don't forget the classroom. For better and sometimes for worse, the academy does play a role in keeping poetry alive. Beyond the classroom, yes, I do know outsiders who love to read poetry – but only a few. One of them is a high-profile newspaper editor in Toronto who left school at about fifteen and discovered the joy of poetry in his forties.

**Who is your audience?**

For poetry, I wish I knew – obviously the audience is small. For journalism, it's much wider. My children's books and especially my non-fiction books have led to fascinating responses from readers in many places. This is one of the great pleasures of being a writer, and it's sad that it happens so rarely for most poets.

**What kinds of fascinating responses?**

I'll give you a couple of examples. They show the amazing kinds of connections that a book can provoke. *Spoken Here* looks at the struggle of minority languages to survive in many countries. After it came out I had an e-mail from a woman who wrote: "I was travelling in southwestern China – Yunnan province – in the ancient Naxi city of Lijiang. The Naxi have the world's only remaining pictograph writing system, as I recall. I saw samples of it at their museums. It's dying out, under relentless pressure for Sinification. I met an old man who is one of the last to speak, read and write Naxi. He and his daughter ran a little language school. Problem: they had to eat, so they needed to charge for the classes. Of course the Naxi are poor, so this was a problem. His enrollment, in other words,

EACH POEM IS A RARE GIFT –
I NEARLY ALWAYS WORK ON ONE AT A TIME.

was pretty small." She wanted to know if I could suggest grants or other ways of getting money to the school, so as to help that particular culture survive.

I also remember an exchange I had with a Jewish man from New Mexico. He wanted to tell me about the Pueblo languages in his region and especially about his grandfather, who would hear Spanish being spoken in his seniors' residence and mistake it for the almost extinct Jewish language of Ladino. The man wrote, "I remember going for walks with him in the park (I was seven or eight) while he considered the appropriateness of particular Hebrew words to express the shimmer of leaves in the sun."

## Do you write with the intention of "growing a manuscript" or do you work on individual poems that are later collected into a book?

Each poem is a rare gift – I nearly always work on one at a time. "Growing a manuscript" sounds like growing a fir tree, and I'm not a hobby farmer.

The only exception I can think of involves a recent poem, "Tibet, 1959-   ." The short dash and the long space are deliberate. My first collection contained a poem called "Lhasa, 1950," about the Dalai Lama's boyhood in a Tibet on the cusp of invasion. My second collection contained a poem I've now revised and retitled "Amdo, 1938," Amdo being a region of northeastern Tibet where the Dalai Lama was born. Formally these two poems are quite different but they're similar in spirit, and when I was beginning to prepare a New and Selected, I thought it might be interesting to create a kind of informal trilogy, the final part embodying the desolation and grief of Tibet ever since the Chinese invasion. Of course it's easy to *say* "desolation and grief." It's not so easy to write a good poem embodying those qualities.

## What is the toughest part of writing for you?

Writing non-fiction is not particularly tough, to be honest. But with poetry, I have to give myself the gifts of space, of solitude, of energy, of liberty, and above all: of time. I wish I was more generous with myself.

## Do you have a favourite time and place to write?

Morning, now that I'm late-middle-aged. When I was young I often wrote after midnight. As for place, I use a desktop computer rather than a laptop, so the vast majority of my writing is done in my office at home.

## What was the transition from pen and paper to typing poems on the computer like for you? Did it affect your aesthetics?

The transition was made easier – or do I mean "made inevitable"? – by a terrible decline in my handwriting. My penmanship has lurched into a miserable scrawl and if I take some notes about something, after a few days have passed I have immense trouble deciphering them. I feel sorry for the poor recipients of my Christmas cards.

So typing poems on a computer has enormous advantages for me. You could call it an act of clarity. I don't think it has had much influence on the visual style of my work, but I suspect it has had an impact on the editing. *Blue Sand, Blue Moon,* my first collection of poems, came out in 1988, and although I was using a computer by then, nearly all the poems had been drafted by hand. When I look back on those poems, I'm sometimes disappointed in myself for what seem like moments of laziness. The poems I write in the 21$^{st}$ century are no more inspired, indeed perhaps they're a lot less inspired, but I'm confident they're better edited.

## Does your day job impact on your writing?

Of course; how could it not? If I didn't have to earn a living, I would have been – would still be, even now – a much more prolific poet. I spend my days working with words and, as Rilke warned in his *Letters to a Young Poet*, this can be profoundly damaging to the imagination.

## Is travel important to your writing?

I love to travel, and find it a great inspiration. It tears some of the fog away from my clouded sight. Often a journey will provide the catalyst for a poem, and the first few drafts will be scribbled by hand on whatever paper is available. Later I'll revise the poem at home.

Beyond that, I think travelling serves to inspire my poetry because when I'm away from home, by definition I'm not editing anyone else's work and I'm not writing a language column. On the road my imagination doesn't get drained away by the demands of journalism or editing.

## Do you write about Quebec?

"About" is a more difficult word than it seems. I don't write political poems about Quebec. I did once write a poem entitled "Montreal," but its deepest inspiration was a great poem by William Blake, "London." In my own mind, the setting for my poem "A Key That Opens on the Night" is a park and a street near where I live in Pointe-Claire. But a reader doesn't need to know that. Given the literary prejudice against the suburbs, it's probably a good thing I kept the setting vague.

The basis of another poem, "White on White," came to me one morning while I was walking along Lakeshore Road. But the poem is not about its setting. I'm sure a writer's place of residence does affect his or her work – though not necessarily in a conscious or overt way. So even if I don't set out to write about Quebec, the place informs my poetry.

## How about other influences? What is your idea of a muse?

On my office door there's a New Yorker cartoon of a bearded man hunched over an old-fashioned typewriter, near a wastebasket containing many crumpled sheets of paper. Behind the man is sitting his muse, a lyre at her feet. She's holding a revolver. She's pointing it at the man's back. ■

MARK ABLEY

## Labrador

*For Annie*

A gravel road to the sea.
A raw wind. The end of a world.

A pile of scanty earth heaped with rocks.

Under the pile, just off the road, the skeleton
of a boy buried face down, a flat
stone across his lower back,
and to give him hope on his journey
a walrus tusk, some red pigment, a flute
sculpted from a bird's bone
and the toggled point of a harpoon.

A deserted beach, the morning after rain,
sliced by a stream through the sand.

Fragments of a warship near a lighthouse
the colour of ice beyond
a village of seven.
               Seven thousand
years ago, who wrapped his body
in bark and animal skins
and placed his head toward the falling sun?
Who lit the fires beside him and cooked food?

No walruses now. No right whales.
No smoke curling over the valley.
The end of a world. A raw wind.

A sandpiper's tracks along the shore.

## White on White

*Energy is Eternal Delight,* said Mr. Blake

now I face a February morning by a lake
below a gull at work in the delighted air

as the wet snow settles, flake by flake,
onto melting ridges that sketch a line of jagged
puddles in the churning, half-solid water

soon, I think, the weather will have to break
but soon means nothing to this granite wind
or the dour, unbroken mass of clouds transforming
the far shore to a moist abstraction

luckily the mirrored pier declines to fall
though its legs look akilter, a cubist slushpile,
ice and former ice in a cracked reflection

a watercolour still life that keeps on shifting
while a frozen artist tries to freeze the action

and the ghost of Mr. Blake cries satisfaction

# Erín Moure

Montreal poet Erín Moure writes in English, Galician and French and translates from French, Spanish, Galician and Portuguese into English. Her latest published poetry is *The Unmemntioable* (Anansi, 2012) and most recent translation, with Robert Majzels, is *White Piano* by Nicole Brossard (Coach House, 2013). Their translation of Nicole Brossard's *Notebook of Roses and Civilization* was a Griffin Prize finalist. Moure has recently completed a full-length play, *Kapusta*, and in the fall of 2013 her *Little Theatres* (Anansi, 2005) will appear in French translation by Daniel Canty as *Petits Théâtres* (Éditions du Noroît).

***Poetry Quebec:* Where are you originally from?**

*Erín Moure:* I was born in Alberta and have lived in Quebec since 1984.

**When and how did you first become interested in poetry?**

Mother Goose. Early.

**What is your working definition of a poem?**

from Chus Pato (*Secession*)

> "language slips, slips sideways, in the tombs
> through the mouth crater
> through the esophagus cavern
> activates this insurrection"

**Writing in 2000, Melissa Jacques called your writing "fragmented, meta-critical and explicitly deconstructive." But your earlier** books were in a more traditional vein. Over the years, you have gone from the free-form lyric of *Empire, York Street* (1979) to playful experiments with language and a special interest in cross-pollinating with Galician. How do you feel the lyric poem hijacks the construction of identity? Do you see your challenge to the standards of accessibility as a schism in your creative process or as a natural evolution? What led you down this road?

I work in language. "Accessibility," as I've said before, involves what you already know. Once you know it, it is accessible to you. I believe poetry operates at its best, achieves its full potential, by working just beyond what we already know. By seeing what language bears with it as cultural weight, and how it is not just a transparent communication mechanism. I see neither schism nor do I obey standards. I love language and work where it calls me to work. I want a poetry as huge and mysterious and adept and curious and unsayable as life itself. I've been writing poetry now for forty years, and change is a part of the process of my practice. All my books are different from one another. Probably the biggest changes in my practice, as identified to me by John Cunningham, were the explicit inclusion of feminist politics and poststructuralist influences on feminism starting in *Furious* (which won the Governor General's Award in 1988) and the influence of the major Portuguese modernist poet Fernando Pessoa, starting in 2001 with the publication of my translation *Sheep's Vigil by a Fervent Person.*

**In your more recent books you foreground language itself as the project of your writing. What have you learned about language by doing this?**

I just listen, and language constantly teaches me, in great part through my practice of translation, to catch the multiple and curious ways that structures echo, refer, depend on cultural references in the reader (not in the text), and the ways that language calls forth useful ambiguity, tensions, sound effects on meaning, productive contradictions, to puzzle out the complexities of all we call life, ethos, otherness, politics, form, possibility.

**When and how did you encounter your first Quebec poem?**

Is a Quebec poem a poem with Quebec in it? A poem written in Quebec? A poem written by someone who remembers Quebec from afar? A poem by someone born in Quebec? For me, place does come to bear significantly on writing, but there is a sense as well in which a poem has no nativity; it is language. It is in a place, but does not exclude entry into that place from outside. So, the answer is not simple. The work of a Quebecer no longer in Quebec can be a Quebec poem; the work of imagination that takes place in Quebec and is written by anyone could be a Quebec poem. Elisa Sampedrín, who doesn't exist, but who writes, is a Quebec poet.

What your question makes me think of: that the first poem in French by a poet in Quebec that I memorized was "Cage d'oiseau" by Hector de Saint-Denys Garneau.

**Even language speaks in different tongues. Have you found the language of poetry in Quebec different from your language(s) of other languages?**

The languages of poetry in Quebec are beautifully multiple and provide many fertile crossings and possibilities and reverberations. My favourite languages of poetry are in the street – that of people talking – and the language of the street in Quebec is French, which calms me. The language of philosophy, which is thought's music, also arrives to me in French.

**Do you write about Quebec?**

I think all my writing is writing about Quebec. It wouldn't be the same if it were written elsewhere. The work of crossing borders, mixing languages, being open to different meaning effects, displacements, is what, to me, charac-

ERÍN MOURE

terizes it as Quebec writing, in the fullest sense. And I write about Quebec all the time in my essays.

## Do you have a favourite Quebec poet?

I like the works of Oana Avasilichioaei, Angela Carr, Chantal Neveu, Steve Savage, Philippe Charron and the amazing projects in language, bookworks, film, multimedia, theatre of Daniel Canty. Nicole Brossard, of course, who always surprises me. Renée Gagnon. François Turcot. Many others. Stéphane Despatie. Louise Dupré. Suzanne LeBlanc. I don't have a favourite!

## What do the language poets do that you find interesting?

My first "language poets" were Apollinaire and Baudelaire and Lorca. My first real discovery of the work of the American language poets (roughly, the poets in or influenced by the group of L=A=N=G=U=A=G=E poets in the '70s and '80s) was in the mid-'90s in Paris in the 1991 French anthology *49+1 nouveaux poètes americains* edited by Emmanuel Hocquard and Claude Royet-Journoud. I'd read scattered bits of that poetry before then, yes, but this anthology gave me a whole community of poets I was curious about at once (except Rae Armantrout, drat it). I was enthralled with the language and with their use of disjunction to create meaning effects and emotional effects in the reader, and walked around reciting American poems in French to myself as I worked. The language poets of the U.S. are, of course, a prior generation of poetic investigators to my own; these days there are many currents at work in poetics in the U.S. and Canada – conceptual poetry, flarf, post-language,

new lyric, various hybrid poetries, etc., that are intriguing to investigate, learn from and enjoy: Vanessa Place, Peter Gizzi, Kasey Mohammed, Srikanth Reddy, Lisa Robertson, Myung Mi Kim, Norma Cole, Fred Wah, Rachel Zolf, Angela Carr, Oana Avasilichioaei, Christian Bök, Chus Pato, Andrés Ajens, Larissa Lai... I could go on. But I also read poetries of other times, traditions, centuries.

## How has the gender/sexual orientation divide changed the language function of poetry?

A divide? I don't understand this question. The language function of poetry? Just check out a track called "aschenglorie" (Paul Celan) by the band radioklebnikov. Listening to something completely strange and urgent that speaks to you from beyond what you can ever know.

## Does being part of the English-speaking minority in Quebec affect your writing?

Vivre en français a des effets sur mon anglais, vivre entre trois langues (français, anglais, galicien) a une influence sur ce que j'écris, certainement ! Oh, yes.

## Would you say that writing in English in Quebec a political act?

Not *necessarily*. Writing is always a political act, of course. Writing *in English* is not devoid of politics, for sure, in terms of the conditions of production and reception for that hegemonic language in the world. Writing in English in Quebec is also subject to conditions of writing in a society that speaks French. So there are political consequences, and social consequences, to writing in English in Quebec. Yet the actual act of writing in English, picking up a pen and writing, is not *necessarily*

ERÍN MOURE

a "political act" for me, who grew up in English in Alberta. The act of writing in English and including French directly in the poem is a political act, though. The act of writing and speaking in Galician is a political act.

**Why do you write?**

Pour ne pas mourir.

**Who is your audience?**

I don't really think of audience. I think, rather, of interlocutors. Interveners. People breaking with habits of reading to join with me in the curiosity of the poem.

**Can you explain the difference between audience and interlocutors?**

Interlocutors are friends or writers or readers you love, dead and living, with whom you converse in doing your work. People whose processes and words matter to you and keep you alive and sharing. Interveners you don't know, but they join your work and intersect with it as they read and as they make their own work: visual, spatial, linguistic, whatever it is they do. Audiences are what publishers try to reach.

**Can a poem mean whatever its interlocutor wants it to mean?**

An interlocutor can respond, and the writer can respond in turn. As for readers, they drive poems in all sorts of directions, some quite separate from the writer. I can work in language to create certain echoes and effects in my texts and poems, but they are always going to be received at least somewhat differently than I intend. Usually, not totally differently, I think; judging from people's reactions to *Little Theatres* and other books, they do understand, as I hoped to be understood.

**A reviewer (goodreports.net) once said of *Little Theatres*: "At the very least, the book has made me question whose responsibility it is that a book is understood once it's put out into the world." He felt he couldn't see the nuances between the works in Galician and the English translations. Of "Homage to the Mineral of Cabbage" in particular he said he understood "the feeling and sentiment" but didn't have the "inner resources" to fully judge the poetic craft that went into the making of the poem. How do you respond to this?**

C'est son problème à lui, je ne me mêle pas dans les têtes des gens. Judge the "poetic craft"? Already craft is something that is multiple. The Galician, to me, is beautiful language whether you understand it or not. It looks beautiful on the page. We have so many Latin reflections in English that we recognize bits of it. We can read Galician, it seems. In a way. As children we learned to read by looking at language we didn't already know, and we child ourselves to be with the elements of rain and vegetation. I translated the poems to give people access to them in English, and leave the Galician there for them to see as well. And wonder at. And there is a dictionary in the back of the book, inspired by Edgar Rice Burroughs.

The article or text from which you are quoting (I Googled it and found it) is a panel of several poets debating the relative merits of the shortlisted books for the Griffin Prize for 2005. None of them are particularly sympathetic to my

ERÍN MOURE

work, but I don't mind. That book is a perennial favourite of readers! Its mysteries are enjoyable, people find. And it will appear in 2013 in French translation by Daniel Canty from Le Noroît. It also exists entirely in Galician in the version of María Reimóndez.

It's easy to Google and find people who engage fully with the work I have done. I've been very lucky in finding interlocutors, interveners, readers. Here is a review that engages with my most recent book, *The Unmemntioable*, in an interesting way, for example: http://www.thevolta.org/fridayfeature-theunmemntioable.html

**How many drafts do you usually go through before you are satisfied with a poem?**

I don't count. It takes a long time for me to grow a poem. I have learned to be patient.

**Do you write with the intention of "growing a manuscript" or do you work on individual poems that are later collected into a book?**

I work on books, and poems, and lines, and fragments that go nowhere. All at once. I work on many projects. Not all of them grow at the same rate.

**What is the toughest part of writing for you?**

Finding enough time to work on longer projects, particularly in the first phases of their conception, where time and research is crucial so that I don't end up just repeating myself.

**What is your idea of a muse?**

For Chus Pato, the muses are poets of the past, and arise under political conditions. I would share her view.

**Under what political conditions are your current poems arising?**

My own personal conditions under which I write are, I realize, privileged. I am not hungry. I drink clean water which comes out of a tap in my house. When something breaks, I call a tradesperson who comes and fixes it. My life is simple and modest, but I recognize that I am very privileged. So my work arises under those conditions. To turn on a tap and receive water is to live under certain political conditions. That said, there are conditions around and of me that I cannot turn from, even if I am writing about a stuffed spotted dog left on a stage. Here I refer to "Idle No More." To international capitalism and the inequalities that get larger both within Canada and outside of it. Feminism. Personal memory. Genocide. Loss. My current poems actually are more hybrid pieces that likely are not always seen as poetry. And my current poems are often translations into English of other peoples' poems, to include these other voices in our discourses and poetics in English in Canada. Collaboration interests me. Working with others to create the conditions not only for me to do my work, but so that others can as well, and so we can influence and perturb each other's preconceptions. I'm perturbed (gladly) by issues of nation-building as well, of a need for change. In this environment, my muses: Lorca, Vallejo, Rosalía de Castro, Gertrude Stein, Phyllis Webb, Robin Blaser, bpNichol, Paul Celan, push me toward poems that I don't know yet if I can write.

**Do you think there is an audience, outside of friends or other poets, for poetry?**

It's small but there is one. There are so many people who care about poetry and support it. It enables incursions

ERÍN MOURE

and aids thinking and the relationship between thinking, being, doing as no other genre does.

**Generally, aside from weddings and funerals, poetry sits on the bookshelf collecting dust. What responsibility do teachers have in fostering readers of poetry?**

I've never noticed the dust, myself, so I guess I don't agree there. Poetry is very much alive among the curators, scholars, poets, painters, engineers, installation and sound artists, philosophers, editors, novelists, students with whom I have the privilege of interacting. Poetry influences in many ways, is read in many ways, discovered in many ways. Teachers can open up poetry with joy to students in so many ways. I guess I could sum up the responsibility of teachers as: cultivate joy.

**In your view what inner resources do teachers need to effectively teach contemporary poetry?**

Curiosity and a capacity for delight, a knowledge of how the different levels of language and language behaviour coincide to create meanings, and how meanings move. A willingness to plunge in, and be affected by language. An exposure to languages other than English.

**What different mental creative process does translation engage?**

You have to think deeply about the text in ways that perhaps the author did not think of it. You have to receive it emotionally, look at its sinews; you trace them, you live with them. You work in a border or bridge between languages, between cultures and times that is, at once, strong and fragile, for languages are not equivalent. In even one language, there are differences in usage, differences in connotation, differences in what culture or geography bring to bear. Translation brings up so many questions. It makes me listen, and think, and enter the work of others very deeply, which is a pleasure.

**How does collaborating with other poets, through co-authorship or translation, affect your own process?**

They are both part of my processes of creation. With my co-translation of Nicole Brossard, with Robert Majzels, putting two minds to bear on a dense and complex poetic work is very useful, releases new sets of ideas, solutions, and makes each of us work harder, never settle for less. Working with Oana Avasilichioaei on *Expeditions of a Chimaera* was a joyous bouncing of language, words, laughter to create a text in which authorship did not matter and fell away from textuality, becoming a character that arose in the writing itself, between languages. Oana's influence on my processes also extends to editing (she edited both *O Resplandor* and *The Unmemntioable* and has had a hand, so far, in *Kapusta*, my work in progress).

ERÍN MOURE

I'M A TRANSLATOR SO [I'M] ALWAYS WORKING WITH LANGUAGES IN VARIOUS FORMS, AND WORKING WITH PEOPLE WHO ARE USING LANGUAGE. A BEAUTIFUL LIFE.

Oana is a marvellous, rigorous editor, whose eye and ear open up possibilities and whose sense of structure helps resolve compositional issues that have to do with structure. Robert, as well, is a wonderful editor.

## Do you have a favourite time and place to write?

I like early mornings best, I guess, but any time will do. I don't have a favourite place to write, but I do like being home!

## Is travel important to your writing?

I am always travelling. I work in and between languages and my interlocutors are many and in different places.

## Does your day job impact on your writing?

I'm a translator so [I'm] always working with languages in various forms, and working with people who are using language. A beautiful life. ■

## The Bread Truck

—I was just remembering something, you know.
—Remembering?
—The bread truck.
—What's that supposed to mean?
—A truck with bread in it. Full of bread.·
—I don't know why you're bringing that up.
—Because it's one of those things I remember, you know. It's hard to say
    why. No, I can't.
—A bread truck.
—The bread truck.
—What's that supposed to mean?
—Nothing! It doesn't mean anything. It's a truck, that's all. A truck in my
    head. I remember it. We stood on the sidewalk. Full of metal racks of bread.

## The Martin Sequence (from *A Play in Shouts and Paraphernalia*)

1

A clown comes out from the garden, sits with feet dangling off front of the stage. Tests the fouth wall with a white-gloved finger. Tests it again. Satisfied it is there. Gets up, turns around a bit, turns to the garden and yells "Martin"!

A dog comes out (or a figure pulling a toy dog, or a dog dressed up in colour).

Clown: "Have you seen my mother"?

Wind-up hurdy gurdy plays (dog's voice).

Clown goes over to trap door... "My mother!"

(Cemetery)

2

A guy comes out from the garden with an armful of wood strips (planks) and sets them down. Takes out instructions and reads it. Confused or not, builds a little stage over the trap door, a square stage about 4 feet across. Admires it, stands on it, leans over, looks over it, looks out, steps this way and that. Leaves.

Another guy comes up from under the trap door and stage, grins. Gets out, moves the little stage over about 8 feet. Leaves.

The first guy comes back to where stage had been built. It's been pilfered. Dismay. Looks around and walks off, tripping on the little stage. Stops. Startled. Stands on it and looks out. Happy guy.

(Stage)

3

The dog comes out again on a wagon pulled by a guy. Stops. Turns the dog's
tail. Hurdy Gurdy.

4

A clown comes out with a small toy dog, goes to the little stage on a stage
and marks a square there, a trap door. Opens it and puts the dog in. Runs off.
(Scampers.)

# David McGimpsey

Photo: David McGimpsey

**David McGimpsey is the Montreal-based author of five collections of poetry, most recently *Li'l Bastard*, which was shortlisted for the Governor General's Award and named as one of the "Books of the Year" by both *Quill & Quire* and *The National Post*. Some of his other books include the short fiction collection *Certifiable* and the award-winning critical study *Imagining Baseball: America's Pastime and Popular Culture*. A contributing editor for *EnRoute* magazine, he is the Montreal fiction editor for *Joyland* magazine and fiction editor for the Punchy Books imprint of DC Books. Named by CBC as one of the "Top Ten English-language Poets in Canada," his work was the subject of a book of essays *Population Me: Essays on David McGimpsey* (Palimpsest Press). He holds a Ph.D. in Literature, and teaches creative writing and literature at Concordia University.**

### *Poetry Quebec:* **Where are you from?**

*David McGimpsey:* I am a native Quebecer. I was born and raised in the east end of Montreal. Born in Maisonneuve, to be precise, but largely raised in Ville D'Anjou, where the city's oil refineries are – where my father worked.

### Do you feel that this setting directly influenced your writing style?

Not really. I don't think external setting or physical background affects writing style that much, particularly where one has the liberty to pick and choose the kind of writing they like and seek to emulate. That process of emulation and adoption, outside the town square, towards a place of commercial adoption, is more where literary style develops. So, the language of the King James Bible accounts for much more of the English style than anything that can be traced to the fog of London. Style can't be self-consciously motivated the way, say, one's sense of fashion might. If setting was a determining influence, I would be writing poetry in French. Escaping provincial definitions of style and manner, even flattering ones, has, I think, becomes increasingly true with globalized access to literary output and the more we're not just stuck with the Bible and *Canada: Then and Now*. A Montreal writer is not required to read Gaston Miron or Leonard Cohen for that matter, the way any resident in a cosmopolitan city is free to disregard regional, folkloric traditions. Besides, considering the tenuous notion of there even being a "Canadian style," cities don't have the capacity to impart a writing style even if they wanted to. There are the tropes of being a particular citizen of course but, unlike barbecued ribs, there's no St. Louis style or Memphis style of writing. I'm as proud to be from Montreal as anybody could be of their hometown, but hometown pride does not make a literary style, no matter how much poutine you stick a flag in. Of course, my life and background has influenced my taste and, thus, that undoubtedly tinges my rhetoric and diction: guitar solos, hockey rinks, subways into the city, jean jackets, FM radio, cable TV, a dépanneur with a sign for Kik Cola, that kind of thing – or thin*k*, as we East-Enders might say. But, considering, the tools of rhetoric allow one to create stylistic timbre, I could also pretend I never heard of such things. There's plenty of poets whose rhetoric and diction would have you assume they've never heard of Cheez Whiz and that all their real time is spent considering the flight patterns of the goshawk.

## Is travel important to your writing?

I love to travel and my travel writing – sometimes featured in *EnRoute* magazine and *The Globe and Mail* – is a vital component of my artistic output, not a side job that I do for the dough. I have a strong sense of where home is so I [am] comforted by getting away and returning.

I particularly love taking road trips with my brother through the United States. In those trips I think I discover more about the connecting power of culture rather than about fun or dramatic regional difference. Travel has been important to me in the classic sense of discovery that you can't believe everything you read in books, or see on CNN for that matter.

## When did you first become interested in poetry?

Probably in high school. I was always fairly creative. I liked drawing and playing guitar. But something about the romantic secretiveness of poetry (or what I thought that was) drew me to my notebooks often, particularly when I was possessed of some consuming emotion, which, when I was young, was all the time.

## Do you write about Quebec?

I do. All the time, in a way. I think there's a part of Quebec that is woefully unexplored in writing. The Quebec landscape of similarities, rather than its list of cherished differences (the strip club-smoked meat rah-rah of magazines) invested in the rhetoric of old European nationalism. I'm interested in drawing some attention to the Quebec of highways, shopping malls, rock concerts and sporting events.

## What is the "academic" or "serious" critic's response to your poetry of "highways, shopping malls, rock concerts and sporting events"?

I meant a Quebec of shopping malls, rather than "my poetry of" but I understand what you mean. Setting informs texture and relief in writing but it does not determine its shape or meaning. Tourist guides do that. People are very

DAVID MCGIMPSEY

attached to their localized prejudices and generally don't always like it when you suggest Canadians aren't exactly more polite than anyone else in the world or that Montrealers aren't more linguistically sophisticated than anyone else in the world. To focus on the realities of daily life in Montreal is to draw away some focus from the pastoral mythology of "Canadian Literature" and the argument of European superiority inherent in the construct of Montreal as "Mini-Paris." Of course, my Montreal has its own constructs when used as a location for my writing. As such, it functions the way setting usually does – as a material stage to dramatize thematic concern. *Day of the Locust*, ultimately, is not *about* Hollywood any more or less than *St. Urbain's Horseman* is really about Montreal. However, my work does employ pop culture metaphorical vehicles and does so in full view of an elite society which often prides itself on its reactionary hatred for the life and tastes of the working class. Whatever, the response from the academy to my use of this argot has been, as far as I can tell, very supportive. I'm an academic myself and my work has been written about in academic journals and my books have been taught in university courses. I'm hardly some anti-academic rebel. I'm aware of those who might wince because my work may contain a few stray references to things they find utterly beastly – things like Taylor Swift – but people like that are nimrods.

**Your poetry has focused on pop culture right from your earliest work – the series of sonnets about Batman, for instance. What is it that attracts you to this and what link, if any, is there with the so-called "serious" themes of poetry?**

I write serious poetry that is primarily informed by my knowledge of serious poetry. I have no artistic agenda beyond that and do not apologize for having a sense of humour. God bless those who see the souls of the rivers and who tell us how seeing the souls of the rivers moves them deeply – I'm not trying to towel-snap them off their perch, not trying to write for the masses, not trying to be a latter-day Henry Gibson. I'm just trying to write a poetry that fits my own understanding of the genre and honours my love of the genre. Again, *The Batman Sonnets* are not about Batman but about love. I'm sure my readers get this as surely as Keats's readers understand Keats was not just writing about Grecian Urns and Nightingales. "If you love Grecian Urns, you're gonna love the poetry of John Keats!" If people have a problem with lowbrow or popular culture I do not think their problem is, at heart, a literary one. Of course, I understand there are those whose sense of prosperity revolves around saying things like "I don't even own a TV!" and those people are welcome to their conceits. I'm not trying to force them to watch *Here Comes Honey Boo Boo* or to keep them away from a busy night of laughing at how poor people pronounce big words. I never intended to write to please tea-circles that confuse poetry with social status. Metaphor itself is indifferent: Things simply do not have "inherent" literary qualities. I couldn't imagine a more imperialist way of thinking; believing that a poem about

DAVID MCGIMPSEY

a great painting is inherently of greater value than a poem about French fries.

**Is there a difference between what you do, and say, what the language poets or the formalists do?**

I'm sure there is but we all seem to work at the same pay scale. I would not describe myself as a formalist or as a language poet, but would campaign for either. Anecdotally my work has been celebrated and despaired of by people who are knowledgeable practitioners within those distinctive streams. I'm skeptical of manifesto-makers but that doesn't mean I'm somehow piteously caught on the outside of a Big Enders vs. Little Enders argument. It's not that such a discussion is unimportant but I can't say that's a game I have great enthusiasm for.

**How did you encounter your first Quebec poem?**

I think through Québécois nationalist poems – poems that were taught in school as ways of "understanding" Quebec nationalist propaganda. Félix Leclerc, Michèle Lalonde, that kind of thing. When I first started reading poetry I was exceptionally grateful to read American poetry which seemed more glamorous and mercifully less concerned about plural pronouns. The poets themselves (I liked Lowell and Berryman) seemed to have more psychological clarity – though I'm not sure that's the case, in retrospect.

**What is your working definition of a poem?**

A poem is a material object that is bought and sold in the literary marketplace. What makes a poem is everything else.

**How has being named by the CBC one of the "Top Ten English-language poets in Canada" or being nominated for a Governor General's Award affected your sense of self and work?**

I'm happy for any note of appreciation for my writing. Any scrap. I've worked very hard at it over the years and held some of my own ground throughout the course of my career. By the time larger accolades came to me, I was long past the curable stage. Of course, I am humbled and oh so happy with the notices you mentioned.

**Do you have a writing ritual?**

Nah. Especially not for poetry. It always seems odd to me when practising poets adopt the manners of nine-to-fivers – though that could be me being odd. I can't imagine any good poetry coming out of a process like that. Poetry doesn't quite make sense if it's your only job.

**Does your teaching job at Concordia University impact on your writing?**

I'm sure it does. I'm a teacher and get to live most days in the realm of literary discussion and study. It keeps me among my peers, maintains my respect for the elders, [and] alerts me to the generations to come. It helps allow for my writing much more than, say, working the late shift at a Pizza Hut.

**Does being part of the English-speaking minority in Quebec impact on your writing?**

Being an anglophone in Quebec, I do not consider myself part of a minority. It's not the same thing as being Amish among those the Amish consider "English," not the same as being a linguistic minority cut off from significant institutional and cultural support. In Montreal, the culture around me, whenever I want it to be, can be vibrantly and presently in English. I come from an English-speaking family, I have a computer, I like rock music, I watch television, I listen to radio, I travel, I have been educated in English literature at English-language universities. However, growing up in Montreal I may have been more aware of the English-speaking world around me and, as a result, I hope, less susceptible to anti-American or anti-Ontarioan bigotry.

**What do you mean by "anti-Ontarioan bigotry" and as applied to what?**

I mean the sense that the English-speaking world "out there" represents some ethnic enclosure that couldn't possibly understand those from exotic Quebec. The hoary idea that Toronto is somehow so money-obsessed that it is at odds with the soul-driven fleshy desires of Quebec. That mythic duality is based on very old prejudice. To me, an English-speaking Quebecer is the same as any other English speaker in Canada or the United States – free to swim in the sea.

**Do you think that writing in English in Quebec is a political act?**

It is a political act. Not a peculiarly risky political act, but political nevertheless.

**What do you mean by that?**

Well, if one believes that power comes through the people rather than the crown or the book, one retains some faith that voting is a significant political act even when, living in a secure liberal democracy, getting out to the polls to affirm that power entertains little risk. So, that's little risk but political, whereas poems – even passionate and articulate ones – do not affect political change in a liberal democracy the way voting can. And while the existential philosophy of Quebec nationalism will forever be invested in anglophobic homilies, writing in English in Quebec is still no threat to your personal liberty. It may not get you many friends at a Loco Lacasse concert but nobody is going to put you in jail because you wrote a poem called "Camille Laurin Stinks!" This not to say the challenge to the freedoms of ethnic minorities in Quebec aren't real and whose constitutionality is not worth challenging. Of course, it's all different in undemocratic countries. If we lived in Cuba, it would be a lot riskier to write a poem called "I sure would like to vote in a free election!" than it would be to write a poem called "El Presidente's beard is looking magnificent today!"

**Why do you write?**

I don't know. Better to ask "Why don't you work at Starbucks?" With great affection and some hard work, I found something in life that I didn't completely suck at. God, in his infinite wisdom, saw to it that I was not to be the starting shortstop for the New York Yankees – which is way cooler than "Canadian poet" – but I'm fine with how it worked out.

**Who is your audience?**

Readers of poetry and literature. The few; the stubborn.

**Do you think there is an audience, outside of friends or other poets, for poetry?**

Yes there is, absolutely, but the structure of poetry as an elite industry meant to reinforce ideas about the relationship between literacy and class structure is fiercely resistant to open up to a less precious definition of what the art does. So, in that way, no.

DAVID MCGIMPSEY

**Does playing guitar and singing in the rock band "Puggy Hammer" connect in any way with your poetry for the page? Is there cross-pollination or is there a complete disconnect between the two?**

I think music has influenced my writing in many ways, even independently of playing my own music in bands. I love thinking of musical solutions to how poems go (trying to think of catchy lines, recognizable hooks) rather than just try to solve literary problems by story-telling all the time. I think playing in bands has helped a bit with that.

**How many drafts do you usually go through before you are satisfied with a poem?**

It's so hard now, with computers, to even consider "drafts." My editing process is less formalized in that old typing-the-final-draft way. To hazard a guess, I would say twenty. But, without a full time-capsule research, I have no real record of that kind of transformation. It takes a while though, that's for sure.

**Do you write with the intention of "growing a manuscript" or do you work on individual poems that are later collected into a book?**

I do not have a very soviet mind – I don't write thinking of a "five-year project" like I was building a dam or something. However, in the process of allowing myself to write whatever, and because I'm concerned with the formal logic of poems, a manuscript shape and idea often enforces itself and my books of poems tend to be less anthological.

**What is your idea of a muse?**

Faith Hill singing the *Sunday Night Football* theme.

**Describe your favourite time and place to write.**

In the morning, over coffee, at my desk.

**What is the toughest part of writing for you?**

Writing is a fairly easy job and not as tough as having to get up every day and go to work to feed your family. I work hard on my writing, but I have the freedom to pursue that privilege. The hardest part, then, is to remain grateful for that privilege. ∎

**I would never go there myself because I have the internet
but I hear that Montreal's Botanical Gardens is a really
great place to visit!**

I got my start teaching Canadian-Lit
pretty much by losing a bet. The money
was heavy on *The Duchess of Malfi*,
and I had to work off my losses somehow.

The Can-Lit prof whose desk drawers went clang
for all the microbrewery booty inside,
told me "Who in their right mind would read this,
to say nothing of having to teach it!"

I met all the great writers nobody
outside of Canada knows: Burksome,
McAllister, Fatchett, Stemens and Donk.
*"Mais, vous avez un accent Americaine!"*

I watched nature shows on the internet
and lived east, near the Place Versailles mall,
took afternoon coffee in the food court,
and graded papers "C for Canada!"

DAVID MCGIMPSEY

**Starbucks makes great coffee, internet treachery, so I'm not going to pretend there's a poem which compares to pie graphs because, after all, the last review of my writing commented mostly (and negatively) about my weight.**

If I was to wear your little red square
it would be to commemorate the death
of a dear friend – and if that friend's name
was Reddinger "LaRouge" Crimsonforce.

If I was to express my best days with you
of course I'd mention the shrimp croquettes
but I'd earn my poet's pay in images
of a hurt man trying to talk to a truck.

If I was to go back in time it would be
just before whoever wrote "If I Could
Turn Back Time" for Cher but I would still
come back with a poem much like this.

If I was to sleep all day, I'd give it all
to you and you'd get remarried, remarried
like you used to do! Like you used to chew
licorice red, mon petite square-head.

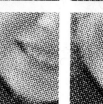

# Mary di Michele

**Poet, novelist, and member of the collaborative writing group, Yoko's Dogs, Mary di Michele is the author of eleven books, including a selected poems, *Stranger in You* (Oxford University Press, 1995) and the novel, *Tenor of Love* (Viking Canada/ Simon & Schuster, USA, 2005). She lives in Montreal, where she teaches at Concordia University in the creative writing program. Her most recent books are *The Flower of Youth*, Pier Paolo Pasolini Poems (ECW Press, 2011) and with Yoko's Dogs, *Whisk* (Pedlar Press, 2013). She has won numerous awards, including first prize for poetry in the CBC Literary Competition, the Air Canada Writing Award, and the Malahat Review Long Poem Competition. Her poetry books have also been shortlisted for the Trillium Award, and the A.M. Klein Prize twice.**

*Poetry Quebec:* **Where are you from? Why did you come to Quebec?**

*Mary di Michele:* I'm originally from Italy. My family immigrated to Canada in the mid-'50s and settled in Toronto. I came to Montreal first, temporarily, as writer-in-residence at Concordia, and then permanently when I was given a tenure track position in June of 1990.

**So your decision to stay in Quebec was a practical one. Are you happy with the choice you made? Has Montreal fed your creative process?**

It was the best practical choice for me. But it reopened my immigrant anxiet-

ies and I have not managed to become a fluent speaker of French though I have tried – that is, taken courses. Here I discovered another way to be tagged and marginalized: allophone. But creatively, displacement shakes things up in me. I don't take language or any single language for granted. I like the culture here but not the politics of it.

**When and how did you encounter your first Quebec poem?**

I don't remember, I probably didn't think of them as Quebec poems. There's a strong sense of Quebec as place in many of Irving Layton's poems, but they're not the ones that get anthologized or taught. Layton's "The Birth of Tragedy" may have been the first one, but really, I'm not sure. I don't remember when I read my first French Quebec poem either – not in school. In French classes in Ontario we read literature from France, except for the Gabrielle Roy novel *Rue Deschambault*, as I recall.

**Do you have a favourite Quebec poet?**

If I have a favourite it is everybody's favourite: Leonard Cohen

**When did you first become interested in poetry?**

I was about eight years old and I picked up an anthology in the library. I fell under the spell of "La Belle Dame Sans Merci."

**That Keats ballad is open to many interpretations. Looking back on it now, was it specifically the narrative element that intrigued you – the fact that the knight gets the girl, but then she dumps him and leaves him out in the cold? Did the beautiful woman without mercy somehow appeal to your budding feminist leanings? Was there something about its "fairy tale" feel? Or were you enticed by its aesthetic qualities?**

What drew me was her name, its haunting music and mystery. It's in a language other than, or foreign to, the English text. I don't think that "The Beautiful Lady Without Pity" would have had the same effect on me.

**What is your idea of a muse?**

Sometimes it feels as if it is an angel, terrible in its beauty and totally mysterious, shaking me to my core. When I think about it rather than get visited by it, I would say that the muse is like what Jung called the collective unconscious.

It is the source of symbols, the deepest images, the dreams that we share; it is language itself, and it is in our DNA.

**What is your general approach to the writing of poems?**

It depends on the poem. Some come out of "nowhere"; the muse makes a free and mysterious gift of them. But most come out of observation and reading and research into the people, subjects that engage me.

**What is your favourite time and place to write?**

When I was young, the time to write included the middle of the night! When I became a mother twenty-eight years ago it was when the baby was sleeping and I managed to stay awake. Now it is early in the morning before the business of living takes over.

**Do you have a writing ritual?**

Not much, coffee and morning light is what I prefer. I read a bit from something I admire; it acts as kindling to get me started.

**How does your day job teaching at Concordia impact on your writing?**

It means that most of my own writing is done during the summer; I do a lot of writing for students during the academic year, the equivalent of a novel every other year.

**You're part of a renga writing group called Yoko's Dogs, which also includes Susan Gillis, Jan Conn and Jane Munro. Does your group apply the term "renga" to alternating accretive poetry, or to the actual classical Japanese form? Why you are involved with this group, and how it has affected your writing?**

MARY DI MICHELE

It started around a little outdoor coffee table at Coop la Maison verte on Sherbrooke Street in 2006. We wanted to experiment with eastern forms and broaden our practice as poets. Renga is the term for the ancient form of Japanese linked poetry. It has evolved and the contemporary term is renku, In our first book, *Whisk* (2013), we adapted the form for our own purposes, including making the imagery and seasonal references Canadian. What excites and fascinates me about the form is the leaping from verse to verse. The kind of connections made are not logical or progressive, but tonal, allusive. Basho referred to "scent" links among others. In a sense, the form is a forerunner to modernist and postmodernist techniques like montage and collage.

I had never written collaboratively before. It seemed and turned out to be exciting. Writing is a solitary vocation, but I have found that it doesn't always have to be so. And what I've learned through Yoko's Dogs has changed my writing style too I think – sharpened the language, though narrative is still central in my own poetry.

**Does being part of the English-speaking minority in Quebec affect your writing?**

I've always been in a minority as a writer – in Ontario too. I am an Italian-Canadian writer. My cultural roots are not one of those officially recognized as founding the nation.

**Does your Italian heritage inform what you write about or how you write? Did its predominantly patriarchal culture shape your feminist leanings?**

Well, I'm interested in Italian writing and culture as it's part of my heritage, though I come to that from the outside too. I was not educated in Italy, unless you count kindergarten! Twentieth-century Italian poetry is under-translated into English. Pasolini is a major artist and his concerns were not parochial. At least one reviewer of my book about him, *The Flower of Youth* (2011), recognized how universal the themes in the book are. My knowledge of Italian, though limited, gave me access to sources not available in English. My current poetry project, *Bicycle Thieves*, in part plays around with very broad translations from modern Italian poetry, what Erín Moure calls transelations. You published one of my Dino Campana poems in *PQ*.

Yes, I am a feminist. Am I more of a feminist because of Italian cultural patriarchy or the patriarchy here? I think the latter is true, as I have not lived in Italy as a woman, only visited. When I first started watching the TV serial drama, *Mad Men*, it shook me up, as it triggered memories of how patriarchal it was in North America in my adolescence, the '60s. I tell my post-feminist students to watch the show if they want to understand the feminist movement. Things have changed considerably, though more change is needed to empower women now, I think, and it needs to be institutionally political, more representation in those halls of power. You think things have changed, then read about those evangelical Republicans in the U.S. and their ideas about how to treat women and their bodies – ideas like "legitimate rape" – and I am horrified that for some in America it has not changed at all.

MARY DI MICHELE

**Do you think that writing in English in Quebec is a political act?**

Well, when Pasolini chose to write and publish his first poetry book in dialect (in Fascist Italy that was illegal) rather than Italian, that was indeed a political act. It involved breaking the law and great risk. I do not think writing in English in Quebec is a political act for me but the "jazz police" may have a different point of view on it.

Moreover, I don't have comparable fluency in my other languages, Italian, Abruzzese, and French, so is it a choice, then? Asked why he writes in English, Yann Martel gave an aesthetic answer. "French is too flowery" for what he wants to do. I too prefer the relative economy of English, and its openness, the way it has taken in and continues to incorporate words from so many other languages makes it a very interesting medium for this poet.

**Why do you write?**

I began to write poetry because I fell in love with poetry and stories and so wanted to be part of it. Love imitates. I continue to write because writing is the only conversation you can have with both the living and dead.

**Do you think there is an audience, outside of friends or other poets, for poetry?**

Very small for most of us who are strictly book poets. But it's huge when poetry is spoken (hip-hop, rap) or sung. I can't sit on a bus without seeing someone listening to songs on their iPods – including me.

**Do you write with the intention of "growing a manuscript" or do you work on individual poems that are later collected into a book?**

It depends on the book; the one I just completed was a project. Some books "grew" to a point where I began to see connections between the poems that I was writing and so I could see how I might gather and shape them as a collection or book.

**What is the toughest part of writing for you?**

The first draft is the toughest, particularly for something like a novel. I'm afraid that I will never be able to write again after each book.

**Do you write about Quebec?**

I have written poems set in Quebec, but I am not a writer really rooted in a particular place, I'm literally an immigrant and imaginatively an emigrant so my writing wanders the world. For example, even a poem set here, the prose poem "Reading Wang Wei in a Montréal Snowstorm" from my 1998 Anansi poetry collection, *Debriefing the Rose*, does not stay put.

**How does travel fuel your writing?**

I don't like to travel, and I must travel because it is important to my work. The sense of displacement when I do shakes things up in me. I also travel for research, as a physical sense of place is central to my imagining. I went to Lesbos when I was writing the Sappho poems, though the poet lived in 7th century BC. What trace of her outside of cultural could possibly remain on that island and yet....

**What is your working definition of a poem?**

A poem is a language structure written in verse – doesn't sound very romantic does it? A haiku is a poem. A sonnet is a poem. Even free verse is written in lines and so recognizably a poem. Prose poems do muddy this easy definition, however. The question I think about and struggle to define is not what is a poem but what is poetry? Music and meaning working together? The clear expression of mixed emotions? If it takes the top of my head off, I know it's poetry? A language within a language? Economy, its fragrance? Many have offered definitions – all can only be partial. It's the white elephant, the gift that cannot be refused? It's the elephant and are we are the blind trying to describe it? I have more questions than answers. I do believe that it differs from prose in the quality of its attention to self and the world, to the moment rather than progression through time, and in the way it uses language, struggling with it, wrestling with the angel.

**You don't mention what is now called "Language Writing." Does this, in your view, qualify as poetry?**

All writing is language writing in a sense, but that term is associated broadly with experimental poetry, writing not aiming to communicate feeling or experience. That's a very slapdash definition for language poetry now. Still, there's a wide range to conceptual and experimental writing being done today. Is the Xenotext project "language" writing? Christian Bök is working to create a chemical alphabet in order to write a literally living poem; as it's beyond our alphabet, it's meta-language poetry. One could joke that he is working on a Frankenpoem but it is a poem, to answer the part of your question on what qualifies to be a poem. It's all language; it's all poetry as I believe that poetry is always trying to stretch the limits of language.

Bök tweeted, last year, I think it was – I wrote it down – "do not confess to being something so boring as a person in love: write like an amoeba, a meteor, or an abacus." John Cage's highest praise for writing was "interesting," not moving. The epistemological is what this kind of writing favours and explores, not experience, not what the rain felt like in the bones of someone living in another century or even today, not the praising or lamenting that has been part of the long history of poetry and what it means to be human, alive and feeling, as well as thinking. That tradition of poetry is not boring to me, and it's not Hallmark card either. Feeling and sentimentality are not the same thing at all. I have yet to make the move to the trans-human, to the virtual plane. Human evolution may be heading that way, but I'll still want to go shoeless in the long grass. ∎

MARY DI MICHELE

## The Blue Bowing of Evening
*After Dino Campana*

I sing the blue bowing of evening
The bowing of darkening evenings
That Kamouraska sings
In a broken down little pastoral song
Among the maples on the dark embankment of evening
That Kamouraska sings
Among the maples on the dark embankment of evening
Broken down little Québécois pastoral song
That Kamouraska sings.

MARY DI MICHELE

## Invitation to Read Wang Wei in a Montréal Snowstorm

In middle age I'm beyond asking or waiting to be asked, that river I've stepped into more than twice: love, sex, marriage and all that razzmatazz. With the ringer on the phone turned off there are no more *mauvais numéros*. So in tranquility I can sit on the couch the cat uses as a scratching board and feel the shredded fabric rough against my calves. The TV remote won't work without batteries. Surprise, surprise. Just as well, when the electronic screen is mute I can perceive a subtler illumination emanating from all things.

Wavering with winter trees, as if written in Chinese characters, black ink strokes on a white and blowing page; in the swirling storm, I too might be drawn to mean something.

Woowoo...woowoo...whistling of the dead. Pipe organ playing in the deconstructed cathedral.

During the Tang dynasty, on the Asian continent, thirteen hundred years ago, a question was posed for which we still hope for an answer: "How do you succeed or fail in life?" Wang Wei answered his friend, the sub-perfect Zhang, with an image: "A fisherman's song is deep in the river."

Wei, I have learned to excel through too much effort and a job in government service. Does it look like winning to you, the terra-cotta coloured cottage? When what I long for most is to sit and listen to song on your river estate? In the thick of the buzzing gnats of summer I have observed old men by the Lachine rapids drop worms from their lines. Though no fish were caught. The men snared clouds on their hooks.

Do I dare to step outside now, in the new year, into the frigid garden, into the blizzard that makes hair white; do I dare to sink into snow, thigh deep? The light numinous. The night luminous, I plough a way through drifts to the back of the house. The wind unwrapping my scarf, an anti-mother, a father who's just blown into town from the northwest for the weekend.

Why do I bother to ask Wei, with no hope of another answer/ What, on any night, can be seen through a dark window into a darkened house? When the storm subsides, when it's calm again, I'll catch the moon reclining in an armchair. She who reads by her own light.

# Gabe Foreman

Photo: Amy Chartrand

Gabe Foreman was born in Thunder Bay and has worked as a tree plant-er in British Columbia, Alberta and Ontario. His first book, *A Complete Encyclopedia of Different Types of People* (Coach House Books, 2011) was awarded the A.M. Klein Prize for Poetry and was a finalist for the Concordia University First Book Prize. A co-founder of *littlefishcartpress*, his work has appeared in a number of literary journals, includ-ing *Grain, The Fiddlehead* and *Event*. Currently he lives in Montreal, where he manages the soup kitchen at a long-established mission.

**Poetry Quebec: Talk a little about where you come from and why you came to Quebec.**

*Gabe Foreman:* I grew up near a place called Kakabeka Falls, northwest of Lake Superior, in Ontario. I came to Quebec because my partner was going to school here in Montreal. I had only lived in small towns before. It seemed a good time to move into the city. I like it here.

## When did you encounter your first Quebec poem?

In high school, I'd read some poems by Irving Layton and Leonard Cohen for class. I remember liking "The Birth of Tragedy" in particular, because it moved so rapidly from one unexpected im-age to the next. Its unpredictability and melodrama appealed to me. It still does. It's fun to read out loud.

**What poets are you reading these days? What book(s) are you sharing your bed with? Are you a monogamist or a polygamist reader?**

I've been getting a kick out of *The Difficult Farm* by Heather Christle. They're pretty zany poems, breathless and surpris-ing. I'm also browsing through *The Dream Songs*, which is also unpredict-able, but darker and filled with twisted Shakespearean syntax. I don't read as many novels as I should. I relish short forms: short essays, poems, articles, and aphorisms and tend to browse a lot.

## How did you first become inter-ested in poetry?

I became interested in poetry first in high school, reading it for English class and also composing poems for a creative writing course in my graduating year.

When I began university, I had planned to study American fiction and economics but ended up focusing on Old English and poetry. I feel like I had really great professors.

## What is your working definition of a poem?

I'm not sure. I like random documents that seem to have a bit of accidental poetry in them. I also like clunky, banal-sounding phrases (look at the title of my book) and feel like there is a funny kind of music there. I'm not sure if that counts as poetry. A nice side effect about filling that book with "entries" instead of poems is that I didn't feel like I was declaring anything about what a poem was supposed to be. It seemed a nice way to step aside from the poetics debate and just play around with sounds and meaning.

## Why do you write?

I don't know. I like deep thoughts, the weirdness and the sounds of words, and bad jokes. I like trying to mix these things together.

## What is your approach to writing a poem: inspiration-driven, structural, social, thematic... ?

All of the above? I feel like it changes between things I write. Sometimes it starts with a concept or an idea that I want to explore. Sometimes it starts with a line or a phrase which I try to build a poem around. I don't feel like my motives are consistent. All of the above.

## Do you have a writing ritual?

Not really. I always seem to have a million pens nearby. I guess in case hundreds of thousands of them run dry. It makes no sense. Is having far too many pens a ritual?

## Who is your audience?

I'm not sure. One thing I like about the concept of *A Complete Encyclopedia of Different Types of People* is that it has a blunt sort of comedy built into the title. It *must* be an overstatement. I was hoping that this could appeal to people who are skeptical about whether things like types of people and completeness really exist. I was also hoping that people might grab the book by mistake, thinking that it would help them to classify friends, neighbours and strangers – and thereby improve their lives.

## Is there an audience, outside of friends or other poets, for poetry?

I think so. I'm continuously meeting people who are at least occasional readers of poetry. There is an amorphous societal interest in poetry. A lot of people are moved by poems, even if they don't read them very often.

## Your work is not readily accessible to a general readership because you tightrope walk between the recognizable "realist" poetry and the "disjointed dadaist/language" approach. One example is from Innocent Bystanders: "I felt a sudden pang. Just a mayfly/trying to crawl inside my trenchcoat./I wore that bug's humanity like a badge." What part of our poetic consciousness are you trying to reach with this kind of imagery?

Questions of accessibility interest me. I guess my hope was that the humorous bits in the entries would render the oblique poetic stuff more accessible, or at least dismissible, under the auspices of it being just a joke anyway. Perhaps I am fooling myself, but I wanted to take poetry seriously and not very seriously at the

GABE FOREMAN

same time. In a way, if a poem contains a little gag, you can leave it as a joke and not worry whether or not you are really "getting" it in a way that people sometimes worry if they are "getting" a poem. It seemed like a good counter-current to include in something as ostensibly complete as this encyclopedia: making fun of the desire to "get" everything.

That mayfly example seems mostly literal to me (at least I took it that way), until the last part, which I suppose is a metaphor about bugs being like people. They breed and die as we do. We stand on the sidelines of each other's tragedies, probably without noticing. To me, this passage is about noticing.

### How many drafts do you usually go through before you are satisfied with a poem?

I'm not sure when one draft becomes the next. Sometimes I make changes to fragments for months and months, but I don't really feel like I'm planking down successive versions. When I work on something, it feels more like I'm making little changes to a single ongoing draft. In general, I'm slow when it comes to poems, I take a long time to finish them, and I don't typically keep a good record of different versions. I have a group of three friends who are also fierce editors and awesome writers; usually I don't feel that a poem is finished until I get their feedback.

### Can you give us a concrete example of your creative process?

Here is a piece that I don't feel is finished, but that someday may be finished. To be frank, I question many of the word choices, especially in the first part, and wonder if the overlapping themes and mixed metaphors are going too far, and if they need to be streamlined. I also won-

der if the ending is too corny. Sometimes, I like to drastically rearrange poems at this stage, or just scrap them, salvaging my favourite parts to spawn new poems. Suggestions welcome...

### Angel Investors

The angel investor sweeps falling interest
    rates
from the banks of a moonlit stream.
She clutches her rake
like it was a liability harpoon
driven through the Consumer Price Index
of a financial dragon. Since she was a girl
the angel investor had been warned
her kindness would be crippled
by the cost of crude.

The leaves being swept away,
are not in possession of why they
have been cast aside by their creator.
It's a part of growing up deciduous.
It's Catholic, but different.
The biosphere is their diocese.
Let the bottomless autumn night
decide what's right.
When the moon hits your eye
like the 'C' in C.P.I., that's amoral.

### Do you write with the intention of "growing a manuscript" or do you work on individual poems that are later collected into a book?

A Complete Encyclopedia had a few little constraints (like the alphabetical, types-of-people titles and the cross-referencing) that made me consider each poem in the context of the larger project while I was working on it. To make it a literal "work of reference," I attempted to make the separate entries share minor textual "references" to one another. The project evolved into more of a connected man-

GABE FOREMAN

uscript than a collection. Since then, I've been mostly writing isolated things.

## What is the toughest part of writing for you?

Starting. I don't know why. It's usually fun once I start. What am I afraid of?

## What is your idea of a muse?

Probably reading other poems is a muse. It triggers reactions, new ideas about things. It makes me want to write my own.

## How important is humour for you in your poetry and why?

I guess for the reason mentioned above, I like to imagine that humour can make poems more accessible by defusing some of the highfalutin baggage that certain people attach to poetry and make the whole poetry thing a little more relaxed, even if the poem is full of ideas or images that I take very seriously. In a way, I'm a sucker for contrast. I feel like starting a poem in a serious vein and ending it with a bit of a joke (or vice versa) represents some kind of aesthetic ideal. It's serious, but it's not only serious. Maybe it's funny, but hopefully it isn't *only* funny.

## What is your favourite time and place to write?

Usually I work best at night, indoors, at a desk. Lately, I enjoy writing on paper more than I like composing on the computer screen, although I do both. Sometimes I write in a tent, in daylight.

## Does your day job impact on your writing?

Yes, I think so. I work in a soup kitchen where I deal with lots of food. Most of the weird culinary combinations mentioned in *A Complete Encyclopedia* (like yams and chives served with Pepsi) derive from spending too much time in the culinary wilds north of Place des Arts.

## Do you like to travel?

I do like to travel but I never go anywhere. I can't explain it.

## Do you write about Quebec?

Until now, I haven't used many place names in my poems to indicate where they take place. For instance, I thought that the geography in *A Complete Encyclopedia* should consist mostly of generic places, like an unnamed forest beside an unnamed lake. Currently, I'm spreading my wings a little and taking on a poem that compares the infrastructure of present-day Montreal to The Doors in 1967.

## Do you think that being part of the English-speaking minority in Quebec affects your writing?

Maybe a little bit, simply because French is not "fluent" to me. On a poster, for example, the French language stands out more like an abstract system of signs to me than English usually does. The message in English gets into my head before I can really notice the linguistic tricks that put it there. Living outside of one's first language makes language stand out more as language. It's more opaque, more noticeable in its details. This abstraction grafts itself onto writing, so that I feel like I am writing in a language, somewhat artificially, not just pouring pure thoughts or images onto the page.

## Would you say that writing in English in Quebec is a political act?

I'm sure it could be, but for me personally, it's not political. English is my first language and I live here now. If I didn't write poetry in English, how would I pay the bills? ∎

## Break on through

Don't look inside yourself
for the 720 exit.
You're naked, tiled and retro,
smoky like the metro,
full of protest and promise,
a buried work of sculpture.

Never fall in love
with the Jacques Cartier bridge.
These things
lead nowhere.

Cracks in every overpass
are serpent gateways
to the other side.

We ride these snakes
no matter where they take us,
no matter how Jim Morrison
this makes us.

Built for 1967, The Doors were magical
and falling apart.
The Doors were Montreal.

## Socialites

At the lamp store asking for a lamp,
do you have any lamps
that don't work?
I need to replace a light which never worked
that I smashed when I was dying.

I have but one lamp
that doesn't work
but it comes with a curse.
Are you willing to buy it
before I start to blab about the curse,
a hex both banal and morose?

Of course
I paid an exorbitant price
for when I took my new lamp home
and set it in the old light's nook,
before I stooped to plug it in,
it worked.

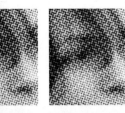

# Catherine Kidd

**Catherine Kidd is author of the novel *Missing the Ark* and two poetry collections, *Sea Peach* and *Bipolar bear*. *Sea Peach* is also a critically acclaimed solo show, which toured to venues including the *Spier Arts Poetry Festival* (Cape Town, South Africa), a Yellowknife storytelling festival, Singapore's *Esplanade on the Bay*, and Toronto Harbourfront's *World Stage*. A graduate of Concordia University's M.A. program in Creative Writing, Catherine has taught Fiction at Concordia, as well as workshops through the Quebec Writers' Federation and Blue Metropolis. Her writing has appeared in *P.E.N. International*, *Matrix* magazine, and *The Journey Prize Anthology*. Her new solo performance, *Hyena Subpoena*, was launched in fall 2011 in Montreal. She is currently recording the *Hyena* poems with soundscapes.**

### Poetry Quebec: Where did you grow up?

*Catherine Kidd:* I was born in Montreal, in Royal Victoria Hospital. My mother grew up on a farm in the Eastern Townships, in the town of Danville. Her father had a small dairy farm, up until he sold the farm to go work for the asbestos company. My mother was only about ten at the time. She'll be eighty in December, but stills gets choked up about the farm at times.

My father emigrated from Scotland in 1957. He came by sea, more or less on a dare. It was either here or New Zealand. He met my mother through their mutual affiliation with St. James United Church,

on Ste-Catherine. My mother was a nursing student at the Royal Vic at that time.

When I was three and my brother was one, we moved out west. There was a job in Vancouver. When we got to Vancouver, there was no job. My mother quickly found a nursing position, and then suddenly we were moving to Whitehorse. I remember the white neon horse above the Whitehorse Inn. My father worked at a community centre that used to be a residential school.

I came back to Quebec in the mid-'90s, after living in India a spare couple of years. It was either study writing at Concordia or religious studies at McGill. One of my first poetry instructors at

Concordia was Roo Borson, who inspired me greatly. I admired her powers of observation and her artistry, her conversation with the natural world, the fact that I believed she was actually a poet.

## When and how did you encounter your first Quebec poem?

It may have been William Henry Drummond in grade school. I'd rather say my great grandmother, Hattie Morrill. She was from Trout Brook in the Townships. I never met her but am in possession of the sole typewritten transcript of her poems. Hattie was rural, prim, and Protestant, but her poems outlandish. They were written to be recited at social gatherings, and allegedly based on "strange dreams":

> I dreamed that Esther killed a cat
> Now, there is nothing strange in that,
> But oh! The way she did the crime
> Sent shivers up and down my spine...

The poem goes on to describe how Esther, another prim little lady, then made sausages of all the cats and served them up at a church function.

## When and how did you first become interested in poetry?

Both my parents grew up in the '40s, liked ragtime and big band, and liked poetry. They both had songs, sketches, bits of poems, or entire poems put to memory. Those scattered bits of verse were environmental to my childhood. Robert Burns. Frost's *Snowy Evening*. Blake's *Little Lamb* and *Tyger*. Southey's *Battle of Blenheim*, and dozens of hymns. *The Goon Show*. They've lived in my head my whole life.

In school, I loved the Elizabethans, the Romantics, *Rime of the Ancient Mariner*, Gothic novels, *Beowulf*, Homer, Edgar Allan Poe. There's a great deal of drama in any of those – many such poems do rhyme and have metre but can also be delivered as dramatic monologues.

Recitation used to be taught in schools. I wish it were still taught, even if no one would want to learn it anymore. It's valuable to experience how verses can become hardwired to your head – they become body parts – taking on deepening or differing meaning over time.

## What is your working definition of a poem?

A poem is a parcel of language, wherein sound, sign, and sense coexist in symbiosis. I don't have a working definition of poetry.

## Since a lot of your work is theatrical, do you call what you do poetry?

Absolutely. The activity that takes the most time and energy is the writing and editing, certainly. It's no innovation to present poetry in a theatrical context. Poetry has probably been theatrically presented as often as not, historically. I'm only guessing. Performance may be a way of self-publishing or parthenogenesis. The theatrical trope of memorizing the work is very important to me. I'm fascinated by the idea that it's the phonemes, and not the sense, which ultimately compels the performance of the poems, no matter how much thought and pondering I'd put into writing the work up to that point.

For my last solo performance, *Hyena Subpoena*, I worked with director Alison Darcy; her external eye was valuable and necessary, since the aim was to present an hour of performance poetry with very dense text. I wouldn't want to do that without giving serious consideration to how it'll look as well as sound. An audience should have some choice as to what they want to focus on, from moment to moment, I think.

## How does technology come into play in your work? How did you come to include it?

Almost all my performance poems have soundscapes by collaborator Jack Beets (now Jacky Murda of Barcelona). Jack made an audio track for my very first performance poem, *Core Assembly*, back in 1995 – it was performed in a claw-foot tub I'd painted to look like a Holstein cow. Prop-elements tend to offer themselves like adjectives. I think the trouble is that I have garish taste and can never leave well enough alone. For me, the soundscapes have always been the audio environment where the poem lives. Each is a familiar sound-forest, where the particular poem has grown up. Those soundscapes have a talent for communicating the emotional tones within the poem, and also provide rhythms for the words to follow or counteract. They're also incredible mnemonic devices. As soon as a soundscape starts playing, the words just start speaking up from nowhere.

## Do you have a writing ritual?

Early to bed, early to rise. My best writing time is in the morning, as soon as I can sit down to write in a relatively peaceful house. Then, I simply aim to write all day. This seldom actually happens, but it's an ideal I aim for. Issues such as chores, walking the dog, and employment very often get in the way. I guess the idea is to see writing as a default position rather than fantasy island.

## What is your approach to writing of poems: inspiration-driven, structural, social, thematic... ?

It's a process that includes all of those, I hope. It often begins with inspiration – maybe some amazing species I've just discovered – there's a luminosity and ringing bells so I know something's there. I research the subject until I understand why the bells, what themes are indwelling, what's so captivating. Usually, there's some useful metaphor for the human condition, which is when the poem becomes about social content or message.

## Does being part of the English-speaking minority in Quebec affect your writing?

Not consciously, but probably. Considering my love of travel, I'm likely most comfortable feeling slightly alien to a place. It's odd because I was born here, but home is a complicated issue for me. Home is where the heart is – I believe – whatever that means. It needs to be a very flexible muscle.

## Do you think that writing in English in Quebec is a political act?

I think that writing is a political act.

## Why do you write?

Please accept reasons "a" through "f":

a) Holding out that art is a way to preserve the humanity of humanity.
b) I like puzzles.
c) "To create verbal worlds"*
d) Long ago realized I may as well choose what is compulsive anyhow.
e) Must ventilate head full of words.
f) Someone might know what I mean; this might help both of us.

CATHERINE KIDD

One would hope my reasons for writing have changed and evolved since I first chose to pursue it as a vocation, though I don't see how "pursue" could possibly be the right verb there. On the contrary, it has been a way of settling.

* "To create verbal worlds" was one option on a multiple-choice course evaluation form in creative writing, in answer to the question of why one had taken the class. Although many of us chuckled at this option, preferring, say, "to produce publishable works," I can now see it was the best answer.

## What piqued your interest in interdisciplinary performance poetry?

I guess I do interdisciplinary performance poetry. It wasn't anything like choosing a discipline from a shelf, though. It more evolved to accommodate a range of interests and experiences; a long process of collecting and rejecting objects for a super-collage.

Teenage hood was mostly horrid, but by grade 12, I was getting really positive feedback from my drama teacher and my literature teacher, and this was a boost. I graduated with a provincial award in literature and a scholarship to attend theatre school. Unfortunately, I was kicked out of theatre school after first year, though well-liked by all but one teacher. That teacher was head of the school. The official reason was that I "wasn't happy." The saddest part is that I was actually happier than I'd ever been.

So I lived on chai and air in India for two years, and filled up journals, then came back to Montreal and became a writer. Eventually, I started borrowing bits of theatre from the closet where I'd shoved it.

## Who is your audience?

Gosh, I don't know. They're the good people who come see my shows. I'm not thinking about any demographic when I write poems. I write what feels true and hope other people – actually, I generally think of one person, but it's no one in particular – will see something in it.

At the same time, I do choose which poems I'm going to perform based on my sense of the particular evening and venue. I think about the balance of comedy and tragedy, for instance. I rehearse the poems with the particular event in mind. I don't think about audience when I'm writing, but think only about audience when performing.

Just now I'm writing a workbook in language arts for entry-level adult learners. The workbook teaches, among other things, about the communication process – how it succeeds when the *sender* gets the *message* to the right *audience*. So, maybe I should give more thought to audience when I'm writing, except that I probably I won't.

## Do you think there is an audience, outside of friends or other poets, for poetry/spoken word?

Yes. I believe these people are everywhere. Just don't ask me how to find them.

## How many drafts do you usually go through before you are satisfied with a piece?

Many. It's a slow process. For performance poems, my habit is to write twenty pages then axe them until I've whittled it down to two or four. I chop it up until I'm left with only parts I love best. They have to connect with each other, too. It's as though I want to first exhaust all my ideas of what's possible and inter-

CATHERINE KIDD

esting about one subject – do a thorough excavation – because I hate the feeling of having missed some keystone or fossil. Then, I structure verses from the bits that cohere.

## What is the toughest part of writing for you?

Mark Twain apparently said, "He has finished half his task who has made a beginning." I couldn't agree less. Beginnings are a dime a dozen. The tough part is bringing something to full term. If they were airplanes and not poems I was making, I'd need an endless desert to house all the abandoned half-done ones.

[To that] I would say that the maddening insecurity of the job is the toughest part, but I realize I chose that and wouldn't likely choose otherwise, if it meant not doing this.

## What is your idea of a muse?

When I'm writing a poem about some species or other, the particular creature is the muse. Everything I learn about that animal takes on resonance or double meaning, when reading science as though it were also poetry. The creature as sacred source of inspiration, speaking through a mouthpiece who is the poet. Anthropomorphism may be scientific crime, but it's also human tendency.

I think of creativity as a sort of indwelling force that infuses living things, and of creation as its ongoing interplay.

There's another more general sense of a muse – a state of grace I can either be in or out of, with regards to inspiration. One per cent of the time, there are magic wings attached to writing and it speeds along in perfect synchronicity with one's own life; the effect is a bit uncanny. Most of the time, however, it's more like the Sunday crossword than winged words; you just have to sit and figure it out, however long that takes.

## Is travel important to your writing?

I love to travel. It's an excellent education, but you have to do something with the education or it is a waste of jet fuel. I was a rather reckless traveller as a younger person, taking off without adequate resources or return ticket. In 1986, I hitchhiked to Guatemala to join a demonstration in the city about the Disappeared. This was not wise, but I did march in the city with women carrying placards with pictures of their missing husbands and sons. Travel tends to teach you how little you know.

Living in India for two years on spare resources allowed me to live among Indians who were also not so wealthy, however. I wouldn't have met the people I befriended in India if I'd been travelling as sensibly as other foreign tourists. I was also aware the plane ticket that brought me there was beyond the income those friends were likely see in their lives.

In latter years, I've been fortunate to travel to festivals. Here, the pattern has been to base new work on inspiration gained from the previous trip. Following a festival in England, I wrote the Blue Orb poem (*Dream of Friends*), set near Stonehenge. After performing *Sea Peach* in Singapore, I wrote the poem *Human Fish*, featuring a slideshow of photos mostly taken in Singapore. I based my new suites of poems *Hyena Subpoena* on wildlife in Kruger Park, following a tour to South Africa in 2007.

CATHERINE KIDD

**You've worked with students in schools. How do you present in front of a class and what is your role as a visiting artist in the classroom? Describe some of the challenges and rewards of doing this kind of work.**

I usually perform a poem as an ice-breaker, and then move on to something more interactive. I'll keep structure loose, as I don't want to be stuck pressing an activity no one's interested in. It's best if a workshop feels like a mutual teaching experience, I'm not formally a teacher. The best possible outcome would be to inspire someone else – either inspire a love of language, poetry, performance, or generally inspire conviction to follow their true paths whatever those are.

I remember one teleconference workshop with a classroom in Kangiqsualujjuaq, a village in Nunavik. *Télélitterature* was a program through Blue Metropolis – I had the opportunity to virtually meet students all over the province but worlds away from Montreal. The students had sent in stories weeks before, and I'd had a chance to read them. These kids were thirteen and writing stories about daily chores such as hunting caribou. There was a mural of a polar bear on the wall of their classroom; I performed the poem *Bipolar bear*. Teleconferencing technology is amazing but not transparent – it was important to ask slow clear questions, and wait out the delay for their replies. I asked one boy – one of the caribou hunters – when he'd hunted his first caribou. He thought about it, and spoke. A few seconds later, I heard his answer "seven." I've never shot a caribou and anyway wouldn't want to, I don't eat them. But this caribou would be put in a communal freezer, the boy told me, and everyone who wanted to could eat some.

**Do you think that poetry can affect someone's life, or contribute to changing the world?**

I hope so. The sound of a voice that rings true or written words that do is a wake-up to the best part of us. It has been so for me, enough that I'd be life-long seduced by it. My image is of a global human nudging-awake-of-one-another, through the arts and in other ways. Poetry and art in general is truly free speech, the human voice freeing itself, in forms accessible to everyone.

It's true that everyone loves and needs stories, no matter how cynical the age. It's still true.

I think enough of us are awake to effect the change we'd like to see – I mean resetting the balance as much as we can, in favour of collectivity, compassion, love of the natural world, and against global corporate ownership of what is nobody's to take. So, it is essential that we're aware of each other and our growing number.

I was a bit sad to learn that the Canadian *Arts & Culture* twenty-dollar bill, the one with that wonderful quotation from Gabrielle Roy – *Could we ever know each other in the slightest without the arts?* – is being replaced by a new plastic bill commemorating military history. I've also heard those plastic bills shrink in the heat. ∎

67

CATHERINE KIDD

## Hyena Subpoena (excerpt)

*If I could be a hybrid species, here's what I would be:*
*a creature who's one-half hyena, and one-half me*
*And should I be called to testify upon my own behalf,*
*I'd take the stand and be sworn in, then laugh and*
*laugh and laugh –*

In the Kanuri language of the Bornu region of Western Africa,
the word for *hyena – bultu –* connotes one who is unsettled,
does not remain in one state, an individual who vacillates
between strength and weakness. Hyena are even able to
shift between sexes, as well as from human to hyena form –
the verb *bultungin* signifying, *I transform myself into a hyena.*

There's said to be an entire town or two who can do it.
A formidable ability, considering hyena notoriety both
proverbially as well as in popular mythology. The public
image of hyena is generally not very pretty, because neither
according to many is the hyena – with its tragic mouth
and down-slope eyes, ursine lumbering and slobbering like
a zombie Saint Bernard, mournful-looking as the mug of
Goya's *Kronos*. But according to a proverb of the Hausa tribe,
*Every fault is laid at the door of the hyena, though it does not*
*steal a bale of cloth.*

The tongue of a hyena is barbed, like the tongue of a cat.
Some humans being are surprised by that, because, they
suppose, hyena more resemble dogs than cats, when in fact
they're neither of those. Most closely related to meerkats
and mongoose, hyena constitute their very own Family:
*Hyaenidae*, Order: *Carnivora*, Genus and Species: *Crocuta crocuta*,
named after a mythical wolf-dog with supernaturally powerful
teeth and instantaneous digestion, which lured dogs and men
to their doom, assuming a human voice and calling them
by name, feigning the identity of a loved one in distress
just beyond that clump of shrubbery. Not such a trustworthy
namesake to be saddled with, a little like naming someone
*Low down snake in the grass,* or something like that,
rather stacking the odds *against* social success.

And so *yes*, nobody loves a hyena – they're carrion-eaters.
Grave-robbers, shape-shifters, liars and cheaters, with a bad
reputation for repugnant gustation. This, in addition to being

cowards and scavengers. Demons and enemies of the church,
overturning sepulchers and devouring the corpses of innocent
converts. Furthermore, hyena are sexual perverts. Known whores
and hermaphrodites. Chicks with dicks who can switch at will which
sexy bits they wish to copulate with. They operate within the mythical
dimension, with intentions that are shifty and shady. Always changing
from one thing to another, not entirely stable. You might almost feel
*sorry* for the poor guys, but bear in mind the Mandi proverb which reminds –
*It's never wise to show a hyena how well you can bite.*

*Hyena, hyena,* cattle of night, courser of witches
with lanterns alight burning hyena butter –
anal glandular putty rubbed up against branches,
in two tones like Tiger Balm, red & white, gathered
by witches in gourds to light their course, then mounting
hyena take flight onto the astral plane to do nuisance there.
*Hyena, hyena,* cattle of night, courser of witches with lanterns
alight burning hyena butter, gathered in gourds to light their
course – here the hyena is *Bringer* of *Light.*

With eyes open wide and a fine set of canines,
hyena cubs come into the world via the so-called
pseudo-penis of their mother – in fact, an elongated
clitoris of identical dimensions to the male apparatus,
making labour a particularly arduous process, but still
downright impressive, and not well understood,
why the females are packing in the hyena sisterhood.

Then there's that *laugh* of hers, that maniacal
cackle which screws with Eustachian tubes,
haunting the hearer *ad nauseum* like some kind
of voodoo tinnitus. Now a crying baby, then
suddenly a crazy lady. Really makes you wonder
what hyena find so *funny.* Unless that laugh
is a call to bear witness, to some *shift* in emphasis –
from general culpability to a clearer analysis, of how
maybe you've been *lied to* by the same set of standards
that has tried to define you.

From symbol of depravity to source of light and clarity,
what hyena best exemplify is that which can't be quantified –
like Natural Science *before* Wallace and Darwin,
a curiosity cabinet, resisting easy definition.

CATHERINE KIDD

# Richard Sommer

Photo: Endre Farkas

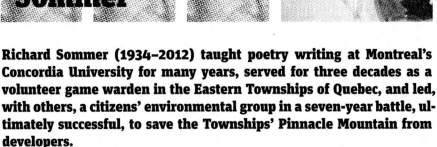

**Richard Sommer (1934–2012) taught poetry writing at Montreal's Concordia University for many years, served for three decades as a volunteer game warden in the Eastern Townships of Quebec, and led, with others, a citizens' environmental group in a seven-year battle, ultimately successful, to save the Townships' Pinnacle Mountain from developers.**

**In 2004 he was diagnosed with prostate cancer, and the verse journal *Cancer Songs* was an important part of his response to this challenge. Sommer lived on a dirt road outside of Frelighsburg with his wife of more than forty years, dance improvisationalist, teacher, and artist Vicki Tansey.**

**His previous books of poetry include *Homage to Mr. Macmullin, Blue Sky Notebook, left hand mind, Milarepa, The Other Side of Games, Selected and New Poems, Fawn Bones,* and *The Shadow Sonnets.***

*Editors' Note: We sat down for a candid conversation with Richard Sommer at his home in the Eastern Townships, a few months before he died. It was late summer, a day after* Cancer Songs *was launched in the big old barn on his property. The interview was a free-flowing affair as family and friends came and went, interjecting their own questions and comments. Sommer reflected on his career at Concordia University, his thoughts on writing poetry, and what he hoped his latest book would bring to readers.*

***Poetry Quebec: Why did you start writing? How did you start writing?***

*Richard Sommer:* I think I started when I was ten. Why did I start? No idea. Partly opportunistic. It was there to do. And other activities didn't seem as interesting.

**Was there a teacher who read your poetry and encouraged you?**

There was a friend of my mother's – Mrs. Olson – who loved the work that I did, though it was lousy. And she died early – died of cancer, as I recall. And I had an ambivalent attitude toward her because she was pushing me to write what she recognized that I could do well. And I didn't like being pushed. So I wasn't very appreciative. But she had a lot to do with it. She figured in my continuing writing.

## Did you want to capture your sense of place and time?

I don't really recognize either of those. I wanted people to see that I was a hotshot. That I was good at something.

## Why did you want that?

I was ten years old, for Christ's sake! I was ten years old, and as far as I was concerned ...

## Were you writing to please others?

I certainly wasn't writing to please myself. Not at all.

## And today?

I just write.

## Are you writing to please yourself or others?

Neither of those. What I am trying to do with this book [Cancer Songs] is heal others or to help them heal themselves. Which is more to the point.

## How does your writing process happen?

A word comes up. So you write the word on the screen. Then when you got that, well, what comes next is something that connects with the word on the screen [laughs]. In other words, it's a pretty random process to begin with. I never know ahead of time what I'm going to write about. NEVER! Almost never do I have any particular sense of a topic or a subject of that sort. I just don't. I'm mainly concerned with writing a poem. Getting it out there.

## Does it feel like that there is one wanting to get out there?

No. You just do what you can with what you're doing.

***INTERJECTION:*** **I imagine you lying in bed imagining the underbelly of the bird (reference to a poem in *Cancer Songs*).**

I got news for you. It doesn't work that way. I knew in a general sort of way that what I was doing was related to my situation. You have to be specific – always, Always, ALWAYS. I knew that I would get nowhere writing a book that was based on generality.

**That's interesting because at the pre-launch dinner we were talking with your neighbour, Monsieur Melançon, about the differences between French [Québécois] poetry and English poetry. French poetry tends to use words like "existence" and "solitude" over and over again. And it's beautiful in the language. But when you see that sort of thing in English, it's a complete generality and so banal.**

It bores me and it doesn't work. I have trouble with French poetry generally because of its tendency toward abstraction and generalization.

## What is your writing process?

For the most part in *Cancer Songs*, I was working from a notebook written in longhand, you know one of these notebooks with a spiral binding and no lines. Lines on paper are deadly. DEADLY!

***INTERJECTION:*** **Does it take a long time to get it just right?**

Do you mean "Do I fool around with it a lot?" I tend not to change things. I sit back in my rather nice office chair, look at the screen, think about something else for a bit, and it's still there on the screen when I get back to it.

RICHARD SOMMER

**At what point to do you go from longhand to the screen?**

That varies. Mostly, I don't stay with the longhand very long because I can't alter it instantly. And if I push, then I get something artificial. If you're having trouble with the lines, then you think about something else for a while. That helps. Not to completely change the subject but to be available to various alternatives as they arise. Opportunistically.

**Who are you writing for?**

The screen.

**Really? So you're not thinking about an audience?**

Sure, an audience is the whole point.

**In *Cancer Songs*, did you have a particular audience in mind? Or is it the same audience that you had in mind when you wrote some of your other books?**

Gradually, I realized that what I was writing was not just encouraging for me but it was encouraging for other people who were caught in cancer or were caught in a fear of cancer. It's amazing how many people who don't have cancer are loaded with that fear. Almost everybody. Because if it happens, then it's almost like, "Oh, yeah, I was expecting it."

**How much of the writing of this book was therapeutic for you?**

That's hard to say because I was just doing what I did. I was active. I was writing and I was writing actively.

**So, not specifically in the actions but in the details?**

Have you ever seen those T-shirts that say, "Just do it"? That's how I felt most of the time. I deliberately avoided being schematic in any way. I just wrote what I wrote. And that worked out

pretty well. If you think ahead to an idea then what you get is an idea. And it's not particularly helpful to have an idea in circumstances like that. You've got to let things happen almost accidentally. And when I did, I got the best results. It would be word by word, line by line. I've written a lot of poetry where I started out with a word, then I thought to myself, "What goes with that word?" Bingo. Got another word. Or a phrase. And it would take off from there. I like working that way. I don't like the idea that I have to come up with a schematic because schematics are treacherous. They can lead you into all sorts of really stupid... boxes and banalities and I don't trust them.

*[Another interjection sends the conversation off on a tangent about Aristotle and the idea of "discernment"]*

What is discernment?

**INTERJECTION: Discernment is seeing, perceiving the particular, tuning into what is happening in the immediate situation, what is immediately happening. And people [now] are appreciating him for that.**

Oh, I appreciated him for that early. Because what was the choice? Plato? Gimme me a break! He wanted the poets out early. And the fact that he was inimical to poets, on that level, is a sign of a basic problem he had with collecting resources from his immediate experiences. His direct experience.

**INTERJECTION: His [Plato's] idea of the model person, the ideal person in society, the rational part, dominates the spirited part.**

Yeah, he's a jerk.

***INTERJECTION:* Not to put too fine a point on it.**

Not to put too fine a point on it. That's not really fair. I mean Plato has some wonderful aspects and I love it when I can get disconnected from what I do. I love the idea of a rational discourse which he maintains. It's a beautiful exhibit of mind.

***INTERJECTION:* It is the occupational hazard of philosophers who think up.**

Well, they should learn how to think down.

**Did your time at Concordia fuel your creative writing, or inhibit it?**

Well, since I worked there for thirty-four years, the implications changed as time went on. Sometimes I found what was going on in the classroom inspiring; sometimes I found that it was a terrible drag. And both of these things tend to be alternating and difficult to reconcile. I don't know. My last year at Concordia was interesting because I gave up trying to improve what I did in the classroom. The result was that my students learned far more because they were doing it themselves and they loved it. It was a love fest. It was a love fest in the sense that they loved me. It was nice to be loved. Partly because I was allowing them to handle a lot of the thinking that went into this without ever suggesting to them that it was thinking. I enjoyed that year. The year before that was hell. Because I was still trying to come up with a scheme that would improve my teaching. Big mistake. And the big mistake led to the big send-off and the enjoyment of watching people think things through for themselves.

**How did you end up at Concordia University?**

I started out at Sir George Williams University and SGWU was pretty free and I could get away with a lot because I had a Harvard Ph.D., which almost no one else did. So my various incompetencies were excused or not recognized. And I went on for years enjoying that freedom that it gave me. Then the universities started clamping down and they realized that they had a reputation as a university to protect. And people were asking for results and were asking for publications and stuff like that. I was never very good at publications.

**But you have nine books now.**

Those hardly counted because when they looked at those, they were books of poetry. Why would books of poetry count? The deans wanted standardized proof that people were doing what they should be doing.

**Did you accommodate that?**

As little as possible. I hated it.

**What's your take on Quebec poets?**

I don't know. First of all, most of them write in French. I've never been competent to read them.

**What about the English-language writers?**

I'm not sure. I always had the feeling that what I was doing was different from what other people did. Not to say that what they were doing was wrong. And what I was doing was right. It was just different. I never really thought of my work as being in line particularly with what other people were doing.

**Can you put your finger on why that is?**

Because I have always gone my own way ... Hard to say.

**Does it have anything to do with your philosophical ideas?**

Not really. I don't know. It really is hard to say. First of all, I am not interested in analyzing what I do. It doesn't work. Because analysis paralyzes in a funny sort of way. And any deliberate kind of poetry writing really messes up my head.

**How do you feel about someone else being the editor? How do you feel about someone entering that space [you created on the page as a result of your experience with cancer], especially someone who hasn't had that same life experience?**

No problem. If they had suggestions, and I liked them, then I would take them. If I didn't, I would worm my way out. I think women poets have more difficulty allowing other people into their writing space, into the poet's consciousness. [They are] much more proprietary than men. For me, it was a question of "Let's get the poem right."

**So, now the poem is a thing unto itself?**

Very early I got the idea that poems were objects. Whatever else they were, they were objects. And in a sense, I had about the same amount of right to mess with that object as anybody else. And if it didn't work, then it was my fault because I wasn't staying with the object.

**For a while you did collaborative work with [contemporary improvisational dancer] Vicki Tansey. It was your attempt to take the poem off the page. How did that come about?**

Actually, it didn't. We did a few performances together – very few – and they were exquisite. They were lovely. But not many. Some of the problems were with Vicki; some of the problems were with me. Of course, I don't recognize the problems that were with me.

**But you were interested in working with the poem off the page.**

I liked doing poetry with the other arts – like dance. Out in the studio, I have a painting by a friend of mine, Rick Bisaillon, who was at Concordia for years, and Rick painted a painting based on a short poem of mine and *that* was interesting. Soon as you get a poem that is settled and fixed, you have something dead. I can't relate to that. It's poems that create questions. Those are the interesting ones. For me, anyway. Other people work with polished, finished, cabinet-like work.

**You mean people like David Solway?**

Well, Solway is a special case. Solway is hardly a poet – in my estimation. He's a workman. And the best of his work is work.

**What about your *left hand mind* poems? How did they come about?**

I think I read an article about a supposed division – now been refuted – and that supposed difference between left-hand mind and right-hand mind interested me because I was in an academic situation in which a right-hand mind was the whole fucking trip. The whole thing! And nothing else counted. And it took me a while to realize that there was a whole half of me that was unexpressed in this equation. And wherever it came from, it came.

**So you wrote with the left hand and the book itself ended up**

RICHARD SOMMER

**being a reproduction of your left-hand handwritten manuscript.**

The psychologists were really into this for a while. Until somebody figured out that the corpus callosum is the strip between the two hemispheres, and it was doing a lot more than anyone suspected at first. In the way of integrating and re-lating and bridging.

**But did you find that writing with your left hand produced poems that were different from what you were used to writing?**

Instantly. Instantly! The first poem that I did became the first poem in the book. Partly because of that. I wanted to have it recognized that this really was a dif-ference; it was certainly a difference to me. Possibly because I was over-intel-lectualizing and had been struggling all my life up to that point to escape that one-sidedness of intellectual construct. So I was delighted to discover that there were two people in there. I got into this, in a way, in order to liberate that half of my brain.

... At Harvard, I kept hearing people behind me speaking in fucking para-graphs. Paragraphs! And thinking what do I want to do this for? Every paragraph was concise and neat and squared off. But what I wanted was a poetry that *was* broken... I wanted to get inside the paragraphs break them apart and give them a different direc-tion. Or, what was a common meta-phor at the time: "Go with the flow." Go with the flow is something we make fun of now. But the fact of the matter is "Go with the flow" was a very im-portant thing for people to understand then and follow. To recognize the flow of life. Not this and then this and then this. And then this. Sequentially or whatever.

*[At this point, Richard's dog comes and then leaves again.]*

Doggie life is very flowy.

**Richard, you have said that if you try to write the poem you miss it.**

I don't know why that works, but it does work. And that is really the way things work in that sphere of activity.

**The structuralists would crucify you for that.**

Why?

**Because for the structuralists, everything must be thought out and be ready for the poem.**

You know something? That is a revela-tion to me. I always wondered what was wrong with structuralism. And you're telling me what's wrong with structural-ism. I got interested in structuralism for a while. Then I began to realize that it was very tensely, rationally organized. I didn't do much analysis about why this was so; I just got really impatient with a plodding system of that kind.

**The book of yours I had most difficulty with is *The Other Side of Games*.**

Me, too.

**I'm still not sure what to make of that. What made you write that and what were you doing?**

Whatever was I doing? First, I was fas-cinated with the idea of a game. That didn't carry me far, however. Except that I felt like games were a special kind of human interaction which I did not understand. And I wrote the book partly to understand it. And I'm still not sure that I did. But I devised a lot of games. Some of which can actually be played. Maybe it was, in part, a reaction to *left hand mind*. It was a return to some form of rationality. If you look at them [the poems], they are very organized. Many are done in a series of seven rules. That wasn't easy to put together because games don't necessarily want to follow seven rules. They might want to follow three or five or... So, it was not a completely successful book. But it did give me the sense that I could go there and... I don't really know what I was doing. I didn't like the competitive aspects of games. I liked the idea of free play. My instinct for competitiveness does not come from that level at all. I hate competition of that sort.

**But you are a competitive person.**

If you say so. I don't know. I suppose so.

**I've sensed that in you in various ways.**

Well, you don't survive very long in this world if you are not competitive in some way... I don't like chance. I'll control chance any time I get a chance.

**So *The Other Side of Games* was a way of asserting that?**

I think it was partly a satire on the whole concept of games. Because I could see through most of the aspects of gamesmanship. At the same time, I was also reading Eric Berne's *Games People Play* and *Games People Play* is a very interesting book. But it disgusted me in some ways because it was showing me a lower order of competition between human beings. A devising of gamesmanship in term of relationships which are not fun. They're ugly. And if you look at some of the games in *The Other Side of Games*... the title is not incidental. It *is* the other side of games. The nasty side of games. You look at some of those games and you realize that the rules are nasty and they have nasty consequences. I wouldn't recommend trying to have fun playing the games in my book. ∎

## razor blades

1 any number of players stand at the sides
     of a dark empty room.
2 as many razor blades as players
     are scattered on the floor.
3 players feel for blades.
4 when one is found, player searches for
     the hand of another player,
     in which he places the blade.
5 the recipient is then out of play.
6 a player who cuts him/herself or another
     is out of play.
7 play ends when all blades are found
     or when all but one player is out.

RICHARD SOMMER

## Postscript

Now it's the turn of others, my wife, children, dog, cat, friends, relatives, teachers, students, the whole swarm of those I have loved or have loved me. What I can tell them, what they can tell me, is largely insignificant by comparison with the two great intertwined factors of the emerging consciousness that flowered here on this strange awesome planet slowly whirling in what we call space – & the flowering knowledge of approaching death. These two flowers comprehend & bracket everything I know or think I know, & the rich emptiness that surrounds it all. These flowerings may or may not be all there is – in any case, I join that all & sooner or later, will be part of it. Oddly, this doesn't disturb me at all – this part of my life has been so full that it would be greedy to ask for more.

My wishes & all my yearning are directed toward the life awakening in those to come. Now it's their turn & I ask them to fill the void with all the riches of their eyes & ears & touch. Be gentle with one another. Be curious & learn everything you can in the time you are given. Reject no knowledge & the world will not reject you. It will take you in as it now takes me in.

# Maxianne Berger

Photo: Doug Williams

**Maxianne Berger's most recent book is *Dismantled Secrets* (Wolsak and Wynn, 2008). She has been involved with poetry in and around Montreal since 1985. Her debut collection, *How We Negotiate*, appeared in 1999 with Empyreal Press. A French version was published by Écrits des forges in 2006; translated by Florence Buathier, it is titled *Compromis*. Her recent poems flow in two directions: in some she explores OuLiPo-style constraints, and in others the minimalism of Japanese forms. Her "Winnows" project serves these approaches simultaneously. Active in both the French and English haiku and tanka communities, she reviews for Tanka Canada's *Gusts*, and writes on the poetics of tanka for the *Revue du tanka francophone*. In 2003, she co-edited (with Angela Leuck) the anthology *Sun Through the Blinds: Montreal Haiku Today*. In 2012 and 2013, she co-edited two French-language tanka anthologies (with Mike Montreuil of Ottawa) for Éditions des petits nuages.**

***Poetry Quebec:* Are you a native Quebecer? If not, where are you originally from?**

*Maxianne Berger:* Ack! I hate this question: Over the years I've felt it to be a challenge to the validity of my being a Quebecer. My Montreal parents happened to be living in Toronto when I was born. Less than a year later, they were back in Montreal. I am not a Torontonian any more than my cousin is a Parisian because she was born in Paris under similar circumstances.

**When did you encounter your first Quebec poem?**

My guess is Leonard Cohen's earlier work when I was a teenager. He was one of the poets whose books were given as birthday gifts.

**How did you first become interested in poetry?**

Nursery rhymes? I was educated in French (my parents were *avant-gardistes*) and at home, I retreated into the English language by reading anything and everything I could get my hands on. I borrowed books from four libraries.

I was given a complete twenty-volume set of *The Book of Knowledge* when my cousin outgrew them. I read these from cover to cover. There were lots of poems. The one that most delighted me was "Wynken, Blynken and Nod" by Eugene Field. Like any little girl, I adored magic and sparkle (I still do!), so lines like these appealed to those aesthetic sensibilities:

> Wynken, Blynken, and Nod one night
> Sailed off in a wooden shoe –
> Sailed on a river of crystal light,
> Into a sea of dew.

I also loved that shift in reality at the end, when the poem morphs from an adventure narrative into a lullaby:

> So shut your eyes while mother sings
> Of wonderful sights that be,
> And you shall see the beautiful things
> As you rock in the misty sea

## What is your working definition of a poem?

Words organized to effect the maximum emotional reaction in the reader. "Emotion" includes laughter.

## Do you have a writing ritual?

I keep a notebook with me at all times. If something strikes me, I write it down. Then, when I have time (make time), I mine the notebook for likely scribbles.

## Is travel part of your writing ritual?

I'm a terrible traveler, but I love being away. My notebook is always with me. It fits into a fanny pack. When away from one's usual haunts, one is more likely to be struck by something as it will be out of the ordinary. But also, being away from home means being away from those responsibilities at home that fill one's mental space and gnaw at life's edges, so there's that too.

## What is your approach to writing a poem?

Words. I like the ways words and phrases shift their meanings when placed in new contexts, as in a pantoum, a palindrome, a cento – and of course, a paradelle! There is always something one could call "inspiration," but its nature is as shifting as is meaning. These past few years, I've been exploring and exploiting the flexibility and adaptability of the English language itself.

My poem "What Bleeds in August, Still" is a good example. I did it in 2011 for Jason Camlot's *A. M. Klein Reboot Project*. The key words and phrases are taken from Klein's poem "The Mountain." My poem is a non-rhymed pantoum, however I don't repeat lines exactly; I change the syntax to have the line resonate slightly differently in its next context while still echoing the previous one.

## Do you think that being a minority in Quebec affects your writing?

That's a difficult one to answer. I think, rather, it's related to my fascination with language, per se, which itself is fed by being in a multi-language society. The politics might be manure, but there is the undeniable fact of cross-fertilization: hybrids can be strong and beautiful. The Québécois poet Michel Garneau translated Leonard Cohen's *Book of Longing*. As he completed each poem for *Livre du constant désir*, he composed a matched poem of his own to produce *Poèmes du traducteur*. It strikes me as a brilliant idea because the closest reader any author ever has is the translator. So after careful analysis of a poem for purposes of translation, one can presumably write one's own poem in a similar/contrasting/response mode. It certainly fits my "try this" file. Katia Grubisic included my own cross-pollination in the "Montreal" issue of *The New Quarterly* (spring, 2008). All the lines of "Luminous defeat: A Cento," are abstracted and translated from Luc Lecompte's book-length poem, *Le dernier doute des bêtes*. I'd met Luc at the *Festival international de la poésie de Trois-Rivières*, which celebrates poets from around the world, and that, in itself, cross-fertilizes.

## Do you think that writing in English in Quebec is a political act?

No. Well, not unless one happens to be not-an-anglophone, and then, English becomes a choice, and because of where we are, yes, I guess, a political one. But for those of us who are born "anglo" – or made so by history – writing in English is merely "natural." Certainly many of the francophone haiku and tanka poets in the Montreal area write in English too because around the world there are so many more publication venues in English. It has to do with outlets, not politics.

## What do you mean by "made so by history"?

My great-grandparents arrived here at the end of the 19th century. Jewish children were unwelcome in the Catholic schools, French or English, but they could attend the predominantly English schools of the Protestant system. It is quite the irony that in the mid-1950s my parents chose to send me to a French Catholic school!

## You've translated a number of francophone poets into English.

## Is your interest in this politically motivated?

Really, I think of myself as apolitical. I did my first translations as a way around writer's block, and it did help. But I also discovered that I enjoy the challenge. Shortly afterwards, in 1999, through an online discussion group, the American poet Marilyn Hacker invited me to translate the French poet Marie-Claire Bancquart for a special issue of *Poetry* that came out in 2000. When I was working with Angela Leuck on *Sun Through the Blinds: Montreal Haiku Today*, I got to translate several of the *Québécois* haiku poets – such as Micheline Beaudry and Jeanne Painchaud. I later translated the prefaces to Micheline's and Janick Belleau's respective dual-language tanka collections, and Jeanne's haiku for a festival she was invited to in New York City. These poets are now friends as well as colleagues.

## Why do you write?

It all comes down to the joy of words and of playing with them. I feel "good" when I've managed to construct something. Some fleeting experience, some unusual phrase, something ineffable scratches my brain, wanting out. Words are my medium. When I find the right ones to convey it, somehow the original experience becomes validated, worthwhile – certainly worthy of my attention.

## Who is your audience?

I guess others who like words. And juggling.

## Are you beginning to think of yourself as a "Language" poet?

I was being flippant, I suppose. Language poets are more non-figurative, expressionistic, certainly more daring in how they write, distend words, phrases, and meaning. I am more of a sculptor or a collagist. I cut away at the chunk of wood or marble to find something recognizable inside. I glean scraps of words and phrases in different places and glue them together in new ways. My metaphors may well extend to the surreal, but I try to be representative.

**Do you think there is an audience, outside of friends or other poets, for poetry?**

There can be, but I don't think poetry is marketed to foster that possibility.

**Do you think that changing the marketing strategy could open poetry up to a wider audience?**

I'm not an economist with knowledge of marketing. Certain poets and publishers are already using new technologies. Online webzines make poetry accessible. Poets read their work on YouTube. Some poems by Billy Collins have been illustrated through animations. But for dollars and cents, I'm really not qualified to answer.

**You're a retired clinical audiologist. Did your interest in poetry have anything to do with your career choice?**

No. Well, not as far as subject matter is concerned. Both fields are related to my general interest in language. However poetry dates back to childhood, and I only discovered audiology in graduate school (I had planned to become a speech-language pathologist and switched streams). On the other hand, because the sport of rhetoric has it that if it sounds right, it sounds true, I do use my knowledge of acoustic phonetics to make my poems "sound right" – through slant rhyme. I want the rhyme to be almost subliminal, not provocative. A sup-

portive rhyme word can be anywhere, not necessarily at the end of a line, and it can be the stressed syllable of a longer word. I know which unlikely pairs of vowel sounds relate acoustically because they have similar first formants. Simplistically, vowels involve two broad bands of energy at two frequencies. As an example, the lower frequency energy bands of the vowel sounds "oo" and "ee" are nearly the same. They are, in effect, two chords of the same note. There is a very close acoustic relationship, therefore, between the words "smooth" and "sneeze." Similar closeness exists between "loud" and "wine." If I want consonance, although I don't restrict myself to the vowel's acoustic partner, I look there first.

**Do you write with the intention of "growing a manuscript" or do you work on individual poems that are later collected into a book?**

Both. Though in the past I only worked on individual poems because I was bound by inspiration, and inspiration has always been limiting for me: Once I'd explored something in the one poem, I didn't keep at it for the sake of a book. However, I recently completed a series which will be one book, and this one is word-based. The working title is *Winnows*. What I've done is to use the technique of crossing out words (a.k.a. erasure or plunderverse) to leave the remaining words, in their original order, as an independent poem. The words are abstracted whole from contiguous letters in the original. My source text is Melville's *Moby Dick*, and my target poem for each chapter is a contemporary English-language haiku. But yes, I do see the future possibility of "growing a manuscript" based on how the poems are generated.

## How many drafts do you usually go through before you are satisfied with a poem?

I don't count. Ten to fifty. Lots. A first draft is merely clay-making. The pleasure of shaping the poem is in squishing it around.

## So you don't believe in Ginsberg's "sanctity of the first draft." Have you never had a "happy accident" where you get the poem down in one shot?

Not for long poems. Some short poems have emerged whole in first draft, but even haiku go through zillions of variations before I choose one – usually by submission deadline – and sometimes, yes, exactly as it first emerged. Here's "February" from my book, *Dismantled Secrets*. From the initial draft in 2001, the words never changed.

> Snow falls
> on fallen snow
>
> filling
> the footprints
>
> left
> by your leaving

I tried to write several longer poems around it – all discarded. I tried many variations in line breaks. So the words haven't changed since the first draft, but the layout has. Still, I had to convince myself it was okay as is.

## Where did your interest in haiku and tanka come from?

I started to read translations of classical Japanese haiku and tanka years before I tried my own hand at it. In August, 2000, after two serious personal crises, I was advised to keep busy. I joined Angela Leuck's haiku group. Several years later, Micheline Beaudry of the *Groupe haïku Montréal* asked me to give them a workshop on tanka. When I protested that I knew too little, she countered with "*Tu en sais plus que nous.*" So I did lots of research. And since then, again putting in eons of library time, I've written many articles about tanka poetics for the *Revue du tanka francophone*. Here I'd say that my work with the francophone writers is "political" in that I'm given a soapbox to spiel about my aesthetics. The notion of a syllable can be very political when writing Japanese forms!

## You've played with other poetic forms. Which have you experimented with? Does formal poetry have more validity than free verse, in your view?

I've "experimented" with sonnet (including skinny and word), tritina, ode, fugue, palindrome, paradelle, pantoum, palimpsest, heroic couplets, prose poem, Anglo-Saxon, alphabetic, acrostic, nonce, and more. Each form has its way of structuring an argument, so I choose the form that works for what I want to say. I consider the sonnet to be dialectic: introduction, thesis, antithesis, synthesis, conclusion. The pantoum is a wonderful way to contrast obsessions, or to expand, comment on or counter them. Haiku and tanka catch fleeting epiphanies. In January of 2001, I jotted some thoughts in my notebook after visiting a friend at the Royal Victoria Hospital. I knew the thoughts were connected, but didn't know how to convey it till four years later when I became more serious about tanka, a form that works through seemingly disparate juxtapositions.

> Intensive Care Ward
> through his bedside window
> icicles
> heavy under the eaves
> ready to drop

The year I figured out how to write it, the poem appeared in Tanka Canada's journal *Gusts* (and eventually in my next book, *Dismantled Secrets*).

As to free verse, I write my fair share! One of the greatest tools in free verse is being able to break the line where it best suits the poem's requirements. So one day, maybe, I'll have fun putting together the best of both worlds – form and free verse – by "curginating" a formal poem. It's a technique I discovered in an electronic issue of *Rattle* in 2011, in an article by Colin Ward. The idea is to write a poem in form, but to break the lines as ↗

if the poem were in free verse – wherever meaning, rhythm or emphasis requires that break.

## What is the toughest part of writing for you?

My problem used to be finding time and mental space, but now that I've retired from the hospital, and parental care involves only memorial candles, I have a lot more time for creativity. These days, what I find most difficult is structuring parts of an article, a review, or a poem. I start and restart, and flip paragraphs around like a hustler doing three-card Monte. Also, the submission process – keeping track of versions of poems, what's been submitted where. It's busy work, and I still haven't found a satisfactory system.

## What is your idea of a muse?

I wrote a poem about that – "Manic Undertaking Spurns Elbowroom." Here's part of the final section:

> My unrecognized
> stalwart's English – morphologically unbound,
> syntactically elastic. Malleability underwrites
> successful experimentation. Malleability
> underlies    semiotics,    engineers
> metamorphoses.
>
> ↙

The poem was picked up by the webzine *Hamilton Stone Review*: nine sections, close to 150 lines, and 600-plus words. Over and over and over, the words begin with the letters M, U, S, and E. Manic!

## Do you have a favourite time and place to write?

Time: when no one else is around, and there is no noise other than the washing machine or the dryer (I find even music to be distracting). Place: my

keyboard; my monitor; my computer. I don't use pen and paper any longer, though I did for my *Winnows* project. I had started it when I was working and seeing to my parents' care. So I printed the chapter I was working from and carried it around with me. When I had a moment, say in a waiting room or on a bus, I could work through it with a pen.

## Do you have a favourite Quebec poet?

MAXIANNE BERGER

Am I allowed to say Leonard Cohen? I realize he's a lyricist. But he uses sound, and he uses it in unexpected ways. Consider his poem-song to Janis Joplin, "Chelsea Hotel." His rhymes are unexpected because they are so different from the moon/June/croon/swoon variety. Cohen's slant end rhymes are remarkable for their subtlety: flesh/left; crowd/around; legend/exception; beauty/music; robin/often. He makes it look so easy, but he also shows that one can use sound flexibly, inventively, and especially, without having to distort the syntax of everyday speech – a distortion so many rhymesters are guilty of.

## Do you write about Quebec?

Do I write about snow? Yes. Do I write about what I see in the streets and in the gardens of Montreal? Do I write about what I see in various places along the St-Lawrence? Yes. But I wouldn't call that writing "about Quebec." Rather, it's writing about home, about what I know. The haiku anthology *Montreal/Montréal* includes poets from both language groups side by side (with the translations in appendices). One of my haiku mentions Mount Royal, another could be in any winter city, and the third, which happens to refer to a very specific Montreal event, has been understood as an ironic metaphor by those unfamiliar with the event:

trading notes
foghorn and train whistles
Harbour Symphony

There are several places around the world that have harbour symphonies. Ours is in winter, outside, at the Pointe-à-Callière Museum. I love its joyous cacophony. But my haiku is "about" home, not "about" Quebec. And yet my participation in an anthology that puts French and English poems side by side might be construed as "Quebec." Though some *Québécois* would dispute this reality, certainly, in Greater Montreal, the French and English haiku communities work together on many projects. ∎

## What Bleeds in August, Still

*after A.M. Klein's "The Mountain"*

Is it still there,
that dark mood of a girl?
Who knows what my heart still holds
rooted in its bloodroots.

That dark mood of a girl
threaded through miles of night
rooting through its bloodroots
for one straggly layer of love.

Threaded with miles of night
all my Aprils there
once layered with straggles of love
now stand stripped.

All my Aprils there,
with you, on Mount Royal,
now stand stripped
of youth and childhood.

And you, Mount Royal,
who knows what my heart still holds:
my youth – my childhood –
is it still there?

MAXIANNE BERGER

## The Makings of a Haiku

*The following haiku was abstracted from the Epilogue of* Moby Dick:

one red aster
in full sunburst
love so near


*The Creative Process:*

~~"And I only am escaped al~~**one** ~~to tell thee." JOB~~

~~The Drama's Done. Why then he~~**re d**~~oes any one step forth? — Because one did survive the wreck.~~

~~It so chanced, that after the Parsee's disappearance, I was he whom the Fates ordained to take the place of Ahab's bowsman, when that bowsman assumed the vacant post; the same, who, when on the last day the three men were tossed from out the rocking boat, was dropped~~ **aster**~~n. So, floating on the margin of the ensuing scene, and~~ **in full** ~~sight of it, when the half-spent suction of the~~ **sun**~~k ship reached me, I was then, but slowly, drawn towards the closing vortex. When I reached it, it had subsided to a creamy pool. Round and round, then, and ever contracting towards the button-like black bubble at the axis of that slowly wheeling circle, like another ixion I did revolve, till gaining that vital centre, the black bubble upward~~ **burst**~~; and now, liberated by reason of its cunning spring, and owing to its great buoyancy, rising with great force, the coffin-like buoy shot lengthwise from the sea, fel~~**l ove**~~r, and floated by my side. Buoyed up by that coffin, for almost one whole day and night, I floated on a~~ **so**~~ft and dirge-like main. The unharming sharks, they glided by as if with padlocks on their mouths; the savage sea-hawks sailed with sheathed beaks. On the second day, a sail drew~~ **near**~~, nearer, and picked me up at last. It was the devious-cruising Rachel, that in her retracing search after her missing children, only found another orphan.~~

(The online source for *Moby Dick* is the digitized text made available by the University of Virginia's Electronic Text Center: the version based on the Hendricks House edition that was prepared by Professor Eugene F. Irey at the University of Colorado.)

MAXIANNE BERGER

# Steve Luxton

**Born in Coventry, England, Steve Luxton has published five collections of poetry, most recently *In the Vision of Birds: New and Selected Poems*. His work has appeared widely in literary journals such as *Canadian Forum*, *Canadian Literature*, *Fiddlehead*, *Sidestreet*, and *Jacket* (Australia), and in *Next Teller: A Book of Canadian Storytelling*. The former co-owner and editor of DC books, he was one of the original editors of *Matrix* magazine and *The Moosehead Review*, and one of the founders of the now defunct *Montreal Storytellers*, an oral storytelling group which performed in both Canada and the U.S. Before retiring and moving to the Eastern Townships of Quebec, he taught English Literature at John Abbott College and Creative Writing at Concordia University.**

**Poetry Quebec: Are you a native Quebecer?**

*Steve Luxton:* I wasn't born in Quebec, but was part of the substantial wave of English immigrants arriving in Canada during the Eisenhower-era recession of the late '50s. This made me one of the last visitors to the New World still to come by boat. I arrived feeling very poorly from the Asiatic flu and actually may have been the carrier who brought the epidemic ashore! My teenage years and early twenties were spent in Toronto where I attended high school and the University of Toronto. I then did a graduate degree in creative writing at Syracuse University in the United States and came to Quebec in my thirties, having got a teaching job offer.

**When did you first become interested in poetry?**

My interest in *reading* poetry came simultaneously with my fascination with words and their sounds. The music of certain venerable English nursery rhymes enthralled me: "How many miles to Babylon? Three score miles and ten./ Can I get there by candle-light? Yes, and back again./If your heels are nimble and light, /You may get there by candle-light." This and many other incantations and phrases – from the Bible, Victorian nonsense verse, and poetry collections for children – made my mind hum in reflexive imitation, while the elliptical and very often mysterious content created in me a pleasurable, dream-like state.

## How did you encounter your first Quebec poem?

When a freshman at the University of Toronto, I lived in a rented room across the hall from a very attractive older woman. One afternoon, I went on campus to hear visiting poet and Quebecer Irving Layton read from his work, including a short piece entitled *Misunderstanding* ("I placed/my hand/upon/her thigh./By the way/she moved/I could see/her devotion to literature/was not/perfect.") Damned steamy stuff for Toronto's mid-'60s, but the poetic vernacular, I believed, in sexy Montreal and Quebec. Later, returning to the rooming house, to my great surprise I encountered no other than the lascivious bard being wished a friendly *au revoir* at my beautiful, auburn-haired neighbour's door. Whether the poet had improved his fortune with her, I didn't inquire (good manners but mostly adolescent jealousy stopped my tongue). Apparently, when in Toronto, he had been knocking on her door for years. She later claimed the famous piece was about her.

## Why do you write?

Apart from the fact that I am exhilarated by language and its effects, I write because doing so employs more areas of my consciousness more pleasurably. Also, imaginative writing is, unlike other activities, not specialized. It can be about anything. So much opportunity exists for freedom and self-surprise.

## What is your working definition of a poem?

For me, a poem is a search and chase using words and their music for some compelling, usually furtive quarry. There it is! After it, into the undergrowth. The poet must not only be intent (though not purposive), but also nimble. ("Can I get there by candle-light?/ Yes, and back again./If your heels are nimble and light.") One must also be prepared for the happy disaster of getting lost in order to find a fresh way out. Employing a different metaphor, writing a poem is like trying to remember the melody (and lyrics) of a favourite song you've never heard.

## Do you have a favourite time and place to write?

First thing in the morning when strands of dream still stick to my eyebrows and I don't always know quite what I'm doing.

## Do you have a writing ritual?

I get up around seven, dress, run a comb through my hair, drain a cup of coffee, and, with callous indifference to almost all other concerns (phone calls, e-mails, tearful appeals and/or media reports that a newly discovered dark asteroid will plunge into the earth in less than twenty-four hours) write five or six days a week for a minimum of two hours a sitting. This can take place at home or in a café. Writing free verse, I prefer restaurants or cheap cafés and "being on my own-some" in a crowd. For some reason, I perversely enjoy being one of those odd souls who scribble on bits of paper in public. This is not entirely a case of "slumming." When writing, I like to be a solitary peeper from the edge. For good or bad, I believe, like many others, the contemporary artist must be an outsider, because more is to be seen by looking in than by looking out.

STEVE LUXTON

## What is your approach to writing poems?

My occasional poems are often inspirationally driven. Though they can also be inspired by the lack of inspiration. The Lord of Poetry works in mysterious ways. Also over the years, I've learnt a number of warm-up exercises: tricks to play on the muse. When I write poetry, I try not to load myself with the intention of writing a poem, though, of course, I am. While sensitive to considerations of craft, or anti-craft, I also do my best to "Zen" the game – unwind the effort as I wind it. Consequently, I am not an enthusiastic embracer of theory, aesthetically, politically, or otherwise, regarding subject matter or form. Somehow I think it conspires against enchantment, which may be a perilously irrationalist view, but preserves the bodily pleasure of creation.

When it comes to subject matter, I avoid being an expositor. I may start with an idea, but I don't programmatically expound it. I *discover* what I have to say. This is also true in the poetic sequences focused on limited themes I have lately been creating – though a bit sullenly. (The granting bodies like this, in their opinion, distinctively Canadian poetic form).

## How many drafts do you usually go through before you are satisfied with a poem?

Maybe one in eight of my first drafts escapes the bin. Of those that do, the average representative undergoes two or three dozen deep revisions over a five-year period.

## What is the toughest part of writing for you?

When writing, trying to express my genuine feelings, and not what I would *like*

to feel, or would love others to think that I feel... and other sorts of sometimes quite subtle emotional posturing. Then there is the first draft: The initial attempt is often so tentative, sightless, and fumbling it is difficult to maintain faith that anything will come from it. Only past experience confirms it sometimes may.

## Do you write with the intention of "growing a manuscript" or do you work on individual poems that are later collected into a book?

Lately, both. I work on individual poems that, hopefully, will be collected into a book, and then, in the extended revision process, try to grow a manuscript out of what I have, while, in addition, writing new, germane poems.

## Who is your audience?

Demographically, my audience is probably an iteration of me. Moderately well-educated, literarily inclined, lower middle and middle class adults with a penchant for poetry reading or writing. Here in Quebec, most, though not all, will be English first-language speakers. Accordingly, I write for myself, knowing that I am, at a certain level, Everyman: In other words, I write for my fellow larks in this noisy, often very grey world.

## Do you think there is an audience, outside of friends or other poets, for poetry?

A tiny one. But was there ever a greater one? In a recent book called *Beautiful and Pointless: A Guide to Modern Poetry*, author David Orr describes how he conducted a search on Google to determine whether people "like" or "love" their activities of choice – an interesting and maybe telling distinction. He found that in every case, more people "like" rather than "love" their hobby or passion, etc. This is true of everything but poker, which divides 50-50, and poetry which, it happens, people "love" twice as much as they "like." In short, the term "poetry-lover" is no misnomer. Something so cherished will always have its circle of pure admirers and participants.

**Does your day job impact on your writing?**

Sure. I am retired now, but was a college and university teacher. The flexibility of teaching hours gave me time to write, though not as much as I wanted. Also, in my case, the subjects I taught – often literary – shortened, though didn't close, the irksome gap between making a living and pursuing a strong bent. The downside of being a writer and a teacher is that the latter occupation can circumscribe one's contact with the larger, various world of work and workers, separating one from the living encyclopedia of human beings and situations from which vital writing draws inspiration.

**Is travel important to your writing?**

I do like to travel. But it is no more important than anything else to my writing. I do suspect that "travel writing" with its frequent reliance on the unfamiliar and the exotic for effect, can be an easy, superficial literary shortcut.

**What is your idea of a muse?**

For me, the muse is more animal than human: It is pre-ideational and, when most welcome, the onset of an almost original consciousness – a bit like at night when, sitting near your window, you hear lone, spooky footsteps dopplering up the empty street somewhere, or, in the country, the rising melt-roar of a creek in a faraway, deep valley. It is a native, primordial alertness. Each time it feels unprecedented.

**Does being part of the English-speaking minority in Quebec influence your writing?**

As a person who, at least from a writing point of view, likes to be outside looking in, I am not uncomfortable with, and often appreciate – artistically – being part of a minority. This, however, is not an endorsement of political disenfranchisement at the hands of tribal leaders. I support the right to equality of political and cultural expression, but, once it is won, also suspect its complacency. This ambivalence is, I think, part of being a minority artist living and working in Quebec.

Double vision can be very fertile.

Regarding the issue of language, I agree with the oft-expressed view that speaking and hearing two or more tongues – predominantly Québécois French and Canadian English, along with a plethora of other languages – makes the ear more sensitive to the mystery and beauty of language. Ah, wondrous Babylon!

**Do you consider writing in English in Quebec political act?**

Yes, in the sense that all acts are political, or are not. Man is a political animal,

91

STEVE LUXTON

opined Aristotle, and, therefore, so are writers... or pizza-counter workers. If I customarily write about what genuinely both deeply affects me and strongly physically affects me, and if it turns out to be the latest outburst of vote-pandering, nationalist demagoguery, then I am expressing myself politically. But the impulse that encourages me to do so is the same as my desire to praise a friendship or love affair. I don't have a less subterranean spot proximate to my frontal lobes from which I can spout political verse. When I have tried to do so, I get hortatory formulae. Maybe others don't.

## Do you write about Quebec?

I have written about Quebec. Among others, I wrote a poem about a French *coureur-de-bois* ("Radisson, the Traitor") who, by switching his loyalties back and forth, played both the English and the French in his own way and to his interest. Was this a coded historical piece about the true nature of Québécois political acumen? Could be. I write about my home when I am prompted in the natural course of events to do so. In my poetry, Quebec is not an intellectual *topic*, but an emotional scenario. ▪

STEVE LUXTON

*Two Drafts*

## **My Late Father's Shirts** (original version)

I snatched them
from their hangers so mother
missed you less.

While, I guess,
I wanted to miss you more
– against my skin.

They were an okay fit,
for a while improved your most disheveled,
farfetched son

I wore them till the sleeves climbed my wrists
the patterns and hues
faded.

– Some might say I squandered
my patrimony...
(From shirtsleeves to shrunken ones in just *two* generations....)

To pluck at the thread further:
Life's shirt-off-your-back, grab onto your hat affair

It was my usual neglect: hot washes instead of cold,
unsewn buttons, etc.
Time stolen for poetry,
the odd passion
you said wouldn't keep out the cold.

Well they helped for a time, Dad.

**My Late Father's Shirts** (revised)

I snatched them
from their hangers so mother
missed you less.

Against my skin,
I wanted to have
you more.

I wore them plenty
– they comforted me,
your dreamy, prodigal son.

But the sleeves frayed,
climbed my wrists,
the colours faded.

It was my usual neglect:
washes too hot,
unsewn buttons, etc.

I was still wrapped up in poetry,
the odd passion you once said
wouldn't keep out the cold.

STEVE LUXTON

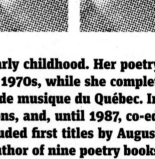

Robyn Sarah has lived in Montreal since early childhood. Her poetry began appearing in magazines in the early 1970s, while she completed studies at McGill and the Conservatoire de musique du Québec. In 1976, she co-founded Villeneuve Publications, and, until 1987, co-edited its poetry chapbook series, which included first titles by August Kleinzahler, A.F. Moritz, and others. The author of nine poetry books and two short story collections, Sarah has also published a book of essays on poetry. A selection of her poems in French translation appeared in 2007. Her poems have been anthologized in *Fifteen Canadian Poets x 2* and *x 3*, *The Bedford Introduction to Literature*, *The Norton Anthology of Poetry*, *Good Poems for Hard Times* (Garrison Keillor), *Best Canadian Poems in English* (2009 and 2010), and *Modern Canadian Poetry: An Anthology* (Carcanet, UK, 2010). She is currently poetry editor for Cormorant Books.

**Poetry Quebec: Where are you originally from and why did you come to Quebec?**

*Robyn Sarah:* I was born in New York City, but that was because my father was doing graduate studies at Columbia at the time. I am Canadian by parentage (both parents) and have lived in Canada since the age of two and a half, in Montreal since the age of four. My mother's parents came to Montreal in the 1920s, escaping the devastation and economic distress of post-war Poland.

**When and how did you encounter your first Quebec poem?**

Am I supposed to remember? I don't usually ask poems to show me their passports when I encounter them.

**When and how did you first become interested in poetry?**

I began reading and writing poetry as a young child, and was confirmed in both habits by my early teens. I have written an essay on this subject. It is called "*I to my perils*: How I Fell for Poetry" and was first published in *The New Quarterly* (commissioned to kick off its "Falling in Love with Poetry" series). It is reprinted in my book of essays, *Little Eurekas: A Decade's Thoughts on Poetry.*

ROBYN SARAH

**What is your working definition of a poem?**

Still working on it.

**Do you have a writing ritual?**

Not really. It's a nice idea. I wish I did.

**What is your approach to the writing of poems?**

For me, poems usually begin with a phrase I like the sound of. I call these "tinder words" because they serve as the spark; they are poem-start-ers. They come to me from nowhere – sometimes they occur while I'm writing a letter or a journal entry, or in conversation; sometimes they just pop into my head. I see their potential and save them in a notebook. Poems germinate from them, sometimes right away or within days, sometimes not until months or years later. I rarely know what a poem is going to be about when I start playing around with one of these phrases. I guess this means my poetry is ear-driven, though I am not a "sound poet." And since these tinder words come to me unbidden, I guess you could say my approach to writing poems is inspiration-driven.

**Does being a minority in Quebec affect your writing?**

Possibly being part of a minority gives me more freedom to be myself in my writing. (As a Jew, I am also a minority within the minority.) Minorities may be sidelined, but they are also exempt, at least to some extent, from the ex-pectations of the dominant collectivity. I think this may help to foster strong individual voices. In the mid-'70s and early '80s, as co-founder of Villeneuve Publications and co-editor of the lit-tle magazines, *Versus* and *Four by Four*, I noticed that submissions from Montreal's English-language poets were extremely diverse, while those coming from centres elsewhere in Canada (Toronto, Maritimes, Prairies, West Coast) tended to have more of a uniform voice – more poets falling in with local schools and stylistic trends.

**You mentioned your Jewish roots. How does being a Jew figure into your writing?**

How does being a woman figure into my writing? How does being a mother fig-ure into my writing? How does being a writer figure into my writing? My writing is not identity-based, but anything that forms part of my identity and experience can, by times, furnish inspiration, sub-ject matter, and perspective for a poem or story.

**Do you think that writing in English in Quebec is a political act?**

*Speaking* English in Quebec, at least in a public place, may be a political act – then again, it may just be "doing what comes naturally," but it runs the risk of being interpreted as a political act. I have never felt that writing in English in Quebec was a political act. English is my mother tongue, and I love the English language. If I were to decide to write my poetry in French – a language that is not my mother tongue – simply because I live in Quebec, *that* might be considered a political act. But it would hobble me as a poet. It would be putting politics before poetry. To be frank, I have not thought about this. My concerns as a poet are not political.

**Why do you write?**

Can't help it.

**Who is your audience?**

Anyone who wants to read me.

**Do you think there is an audience, outside of friends or other poets, for poetry?**

Yes. When my poems have been broadcast on Garrison Keillor's *The Writer's Almanac*, I have received e-mails from many American listeners who were not poets: homebound mothers, an elementary school teacher, a pediatrician, a marine biologist, a parole officer, among others. So they're out there. But I think to reach such an audience, the poetry has to be accessible and speak to universal human concerns in a way that moves people.

**What is your take on the so-called "Language poets" who believe that language itself (foregrounding, deconstructing, unpacking) is what poetry should be concerned with?**

I think poetic ideologies of any sort are limiting. Why should poetry concern itself with any one thing?

**Does your day job impact on your writing?**

It limits my time. And "money writing" occupies mental files that have to be disengaged before I can do my own writing.

**What kind of "money writing" do you do?**

As a freelancer, after I left teaching in the mid-1990s to write full time, I used to do a lot of literary journalism and newspaper writing (op-eds and short articles on education, literacy, and other subjects; later, a poetry column in *The Gazette*) as well as writing-related activities such as manuscript editing and workshop facilitating. I still do the occasional workshop, but since 2010, my position as poetry editor for Cormorant Books has replaced the journalism.

Besides the time it takes, I've found that engaging deeply with the work of other poets taps into the same creative energy as writing a poem of my own. I love this work. It's endlessly interesting to me, but there's no question that it competes with my own writing.

**How many drafts do you usually go through before you are satisfied with a poem?**

It varies, and it's hard to describe. I tend to work one continuously evolving draft, rather than a series of complete drafts. I work longhand (and/or longhand over typescript), making changes on a line-by-line basis as I go along, periodically copying or re-typing the poem from the beginning so I can continue working from clean copy. Sometimes I have different stanzas evolving separately in this way, from different tinder words, and I have an idea that they are part of the same poem but it may take some time for me to see how they fit together. Sometimes a poem gets stuck for a while, and I come back to it later – it can be years later, and it can happen more than once. By the time I write the final words of this evolving single draft, most of the revising has been done. The process can take anywhere from an afternoon to a decade or longer.

**Can you give us an example of a first draft and a later or last draft of a poem?**

That would be hard to do, because I don't usually have anything I could call a "first draft." I just have my organically evolving, often chaotic draft work, beginning as pages of scratched-over longhand in a Hilroy notebook, continuing with pages of inked-over typescript. Not to mention pre-poem tinder words jotted down in earlier notebooks, and periodic false starts at working with them – attempts that may span years. All of this further complicated by the fact that much of the handwriting in this draft work is legible only to me.

**Do you write with the intention of "growing a manuscript" or do you work on individual poems that are later collected into a book?**

Definitely, individual poems. I have never written a poem to serve a book I had in mind. But once I have enough poems to think of publishing a new collection, I do put a lot of thought into choosing and sequencing poems that will work together as a book.

**Do you feel that "writing towards a book" would somehow compromise the quality of the poem?**

Not necessarily. It just isn't the way I work. If I did, though, I think I would still demand of myself that each poem be able to stand on its own as a poem, independently of its context in the book.

**What is the toughest part of writing for you?**

Maintaining the discipline to make daily time for it. Disengaging my mind from everything else in order to be open to it. Recognizing and confronting various forms of procrastination. Resisting dangerous superstitions (such as that if I am not Tolstoy or Shakespeare, I should forget about it.) Resisting other dangerous superstitions (such as that I don't need to aspire to the level of Tolstoy or Shakespeare.)

**What is your idea of a muse?**

I have never really thought about this. That said, there are certain poets I read

when I'm looking for a jump-start – poets who seem to stimulate my mind towards writing poems. Wallace Stevens, William Carlos Williams, Marianne Moore. They aren't necessarily my favourite poets, or poets I'm inclined to read at other times.

**Do you have a favourite time and place to write?**

No, but certain kinds of weather and light help to put me in the mood – the kinds of weather we call "atmospheric." Wild windy rainy days, especially in autumn, with lamps on indoors during the day. Falling snow I find meditative. Blizzards are great. Early morning light and late afternoon light are better than midday light. Does this mean I write more or better at those times? No, but those are the times when I'm most strongly reminded that I want to be writing. And I am more likely to open a notebook and start scribbling.

**Do you like to travel? Is it important to your writing?**

Of course I like to travel, doesn't everyone? Question arising: As a poet, how much can I afford to travel? Next question: Is travel important to my writing? I guess it must not be. In fact, I find travel likelier to arrest or disrupt my writing than to stimulate it. In order to write, I need quiet, stability, and routine. These aren't always easy to create for myself while on the move or sojourning away from home.

**Do you have a favourite Quebec poet?**

No particular favourite, no. I feel a connection to Klein, of course, a Montreal Jewish poet who raised his family on my street, just half a block from where I live. (I walk past the house every day.) And of my own generation, Peter Van Toorn, whose poems and ideas about poetry were deeply inspiring to me when I was in my early twenties. Jack Hannan and Bruce Taylor are two other Quebec poets whose work I find inspiring. I had the privilege of publishing some of their early poems in Villeneuve's chapbook series thirty years ago, and much more recently, of editing their latest collections for Cormorant.

## Do you write about Quebec?

Not "about" Quebec as a subject in itself. But Quebec is where I live, Montreal is my "home place," and I write primarily from my life experience. So Quebec certainly makes itself felt in my poetry. There's a lot of winter in my poems. A lot of local weather and ambience, sights and sounds, both urban and rural, as well as allusions to particular streets or landmarks, both current and remembered. I once wrote a poem called "Québerac," named for a certain locally available cheap wine, now long defunct but ubiquitous in the '70s and sold (if I remember right) only by the magnum. French words and phrases have sometimes found their way into my poems, not because I was trying to "write Québec" (as I think it could be said Klein was trying to do in his bilingual poems) but simply because they were the first words that came to mind – the appropriate words in the context of the poem, and part of the soundscape of home. ■

99

## The Orchestre du Conservatoire Rehearses in
##    Salle St-Sulpice

Come with me now: round to the side entrance
and down the marble stairs,
past the Sunday dwarf who guards the *Vestiaire*,
to the basement hall with its faint smell
of a scooped-out pumpkin – quickly, come,

we are late, you see – already
the bows are sliding up and down
under the dim spotlights where smoke
from morning cigarettes collects to hang
like a blue island on the musty air...

You can write your name in dust
on the wooden seats of the fold-down chairs
where the hinged cases lie open
like empty carapaces, lined in old plush
motheaten blue or threadbare red

blackened by tarnish from silver keys
or dandruffed by rosin. On the *scène*
the *chef d'orchestre*, haloed by wild hair,
bohemian in a new red flannel shirt
points at the brass with trembling stick,

and the bell of a French horn, raised on cue,
gleams a reply. One long golden note
hurts into being, drawn out pure till he
clips it off with a flick – then drops into a
mincing squat, hissing

*Pianissimo!*
(and beyond the heavy drapes, out
on the snowy street, making moan,
the hooded pigeons promenade
to a solemn bonging of bells.)

## Rue Jeanne Mance

...there were birds, they knocked.
flurries from the thin
branches and it was still
snowing...two Hasids in their
black gabardines swept by, gestures
extravagant as the bells
of the Greek Orthodox church
then ringing – when just above
you a window suddenly
opened – a hand flung out
arcs of breadcrumbs

and for a moment you were
lifted
clear of it all, you rode
the watery light upward
like a sparrow

ROBYN SARAH

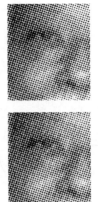

# Mahamud Siad Togane

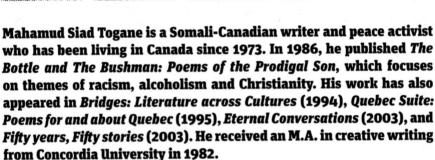

Photo: Madeleine Lefebvre

**Mahamud Siad Togane is a Somali-Canadian writer and peace activist who has been living in Canada since 1973. In 1986, he published *The Bottle and The Bushman: Poems of the Prodigal Son*, which focuses on themes of racism, alcoholism and Christianity. His work has also appeared in *Bridges: Literature across Cultures* (1994), *Quebec Suite: Poems for and about Quebec* (1995), *Eternal Conversations* (2003), and *Fifty years, Fifty stories* (2003). He received an M.A. in creative writing from Concordia University in 1982.**

*Poetry Quebec:* **Where are you originally from and why did you come to Quebec?**

*Mahamud Siad Togane:* I am from Mogadishu. How I ended up here in Montreal is a long tale; let me just say, as someone once said of Switzerland, Canada has now become a country where few things begin, but many things end up. I came here fleeing from slavery like Nigger Jim! That is why I sang in *Exile I* thus:

> Now it is/the seventh season of sorrow
> since I ran away from home
> from my kingdom by the sea
> from Mighty Mouth's cruel laughter
> like a latter-day slave
> to Canada
> to a land kinder than home ...

**When did you encounter your first Quebec poem?**

In 1973, I encountered, here in Montreal, Michèle Lalonde and her poem, "Speak White!" which is and remains the best introduction to the Québécois, who consider themselves les nègres blancs d'Amérique, forced to "Speak White!" I know what she means by "Speak White."

**How does it resonate with you?**

I encountered this wonderful poem when I came here and found out that they – the Québécois – don't speak White here in Canada! Just like Nigger Jim, I was confused, I was confounded, I couldn't understand why the Québécois didn't want to speak White. I could not help but ask Huck, as Nigger Jim had done over a century and half ago, "Why, Huck, doan' de French people talk de same way we does?"

H: That's a Frenchman's WAY of saying it...Looky here, Jim; does a cat talk like we do?

J: No, a cat don't.

H: Well, does a cow?

J: No, a cow don't, nuther.

H: And ain't it natural and right for a cat and a cow to talk different from US?

J: Why, mos' sholy it is.

H: Well, then, why ain't it natural and right for a FRENCHMAN to talk different from us? You answer me that.

J: WELL, den! Dad blame it, why doan' he TALK like a man? You answer me DAT!

To this day there are many honky Canucks who think like Nigger Jim, who can't understand why the Québécois can't speak White! They are "tête carrée," they are tête de farty! For me this poem captures the "dialogue of the deaf" between Quebec and the rest of Canada. But I began to understand the seriousness of the situation when I overheard this joke in Toronto: "Hey how come we Canadians ended up with frogs and the Yanks with niggers? Answer? "Because, as always, the Yanks had the first choice!"

## When did you first become interested in poetry?

As a child, I heard my mom recite poems. And it was just like magic. I felt like the Prince of Boandhere as she sang to me: "Puff the magic dragon lived by the sea / And frolicked / In the autumn mist / In a land called Somaliland!"

It was a splendid holiday from the workaday world. What can the poor stars do when the moon mother loves you, when your mother and Allah love you? I was mesmerized by the MooMoo of the milk of her mindfulness, by the murmur of her metre, by the memes of her meta-phors, by her music, by her mojo, by her moxie, by her monad, by her love, which said to me, as above so below, by her mnemonic mind, by how Mother herself became transformed, transfixed, as she sang, with unearthly authority, with impeccable audacity, with unspeakable joy, full of glory, full of story, full of power, full of grace, full of Truth that transported her and me away from Chronos into Kairos, into the sacred Time of "Would you like to ride in my beautiful balloon / We could float among the stars together, you and I / For we can fly / we can fly / Up, up and away / Love is waiting there in my beautiful balloon / Way up in the air in my beautiful balloon."

It was like wishing upon a star and "When you wish upon a star / makes no difference who you are / anything your heart desires /will come to you / if your heart is in your dream / no request is too extreme / when you wish upon a star as dreamers do. Fate is kind / She brings to those to love the sweet fulfillment of / their secret longing // Like a bolt out of the blue, fate steps in and sees you through, when you wish upon a star / your dreams come true." When you wish upon a star, your dreams come true – with Allah holding one hand, with Mom holding your other hand in the land of poesy, in the land of YES, far, far away from Somalia, from the land of NO!

## What is your working definition of a poem?

A poem is above and beyond definition; a poem is like Allah! Whose ninety-nine names are known by Moslems but the hundredth one, the real one that counts, nobody knows except the camel. That is why the camel has his nose always in the air, majestically looking down at everyone. With a poem I try to name the unnamable, I try to say the unsayable. Like Louis Untermeyer, I believe "poetry is a wild attempt to define the indefinable." And as Shelley perceived, "Poetry is the record of the best and happiest moments of the happiest and best minds…. A poem is the very image of life expressed in its eternal truth." As always, the final word goes to Sheikh Zabur [Shakespeare] who waxes and wows us all thus: "The poet's eye / In fine frenzy rolling / Doth glance / From heaven to earth / From earth to heaven / And as imagination bodies forth / The forms of things unknown / The poet's pen / Turns them to shapes and gives to airy nothing / A local habitation and a name."

### Describe your writing ritual.

At dawn, I try to wake up. I try to rise and shine like the sun. I wake up when I tire of staying in bed playing dead. I wake up to receive my daily word along with my daily bread. On my best days I even forget about the daily bread and grab the daily word to my soul which is "the sword of my Spirit" with which I fight all that is sicko Somali, all that is silly, all that is sordid, all that is senseless, all that is S.I.N. – self-inflicted nonsense – as Iyanla Vanzant refers to sin.

### How do you go about writing a poem?

It varies, for variety is the spice and the prize of life. If I am worked up and am afraid that I will rant and rave, I submit to the difficult discipline of writing to a form so I will remain sane and say sanative words to myself. If I am truly inspired, I let it rip and happily hope that sound and sense will surrender to each other so together they can make some magic, some meaning, some sense. If I am truly obsessed, if I am truly possessed by an emotion not recollected in tranquility, I put it down on paper to get rid of it, to exorcise it, to watch it shake, rock, roll and rattle, to watch it writhe, rime, rhythm, into reasons of rightness. I put it down on paper singing "Tutti frutti oh rutti / Wop bop a loo bop a lop bam boom." Furthermore, I am driven to write if I see a donkey kick another donkey unjustly. I am most moved, I am most dissatisfied, till I write, till I right that wrong, till I kick that donkey back to his dirty Darod donkeydom!

I also write poems demanded by occasions that seize me. I also write when I am seized by the sound of anima mundi, by the epiphanies of theodicy, by the numen of the numinous within me, by the luminous, by the aleatory, by the theophany of the Universe, by the Cosmos that delivers me from my own Chaos, from my own liminal loony tunes!

### Do you think that being part of the English-speaking minority in Quebec affects your writing?

I write White. I speak White. I live, I move, I have my being in White. Going back to Michèle Lalonde:

> speak white
> de Westminster à Washington
>   relayez-vous
> speak white comme à Wall Street
> white comme à Watts
> be civilized…

To which I must add, "O Prospero / O Peckerwoods / O honkies / You taught me language / and my profit on't. Is / I know how to curse / The red plague rid you / For learning me your language / for when Miss Gehman, the Mennonite Missionary teacher, meowed / HOW

MAHAMUD SIAD TOGANE

OLD ARE YOU? When I mimicked what bushman ears heard / in *Abgal* dialect / HAA U RAA YO" meaning "Pray, What stinks so bad / who cut that evil fart / stop cutting up / I shriveled in the shaming laughter of the class / But now right white through the nose I babble pray bray / for I am mad / bad / cad / dad / fad / gad / had / lad / pad / rad / sad /tad / yad / bat / cat / fat / hat / kat / mat / nat / pat / sat / tat / vat / at?

  FUCKINOBASTARBILAADIFOOL!" [Fucking Bastard Bloody Fool]

## Do you think that writing in English in Quebec is a political act?

Why? Because Quebec has no official language: Every official language I know of has an army and a navy behind it to back it up, to make sure everybody speaks White. So now Quebec knows what it has to do to make sure that everybody "Parlez-vous français." My friend, everything I do or I don't do here or there or everywhere is political. Graham Greene is right on: "Politics is in the air we breathe, like the presence or absence of God." The Devil was and is the first politician, and this American white world belongs to the Devil who is as American as ice-cream. As the disciples of the Devil, we are all little squalid smarmy politicians and according to one of my favourite American poets, e. e. cummings, "A politician is an arse upon which everyone has sat except a man." I speak White because I love the Yankee Dollar! Brother Malcolm X was right on the dollar when he told us "It's easy to become a satellite today without even being aware of it. This country can seduce God. Yes, it has that seductive power of dollarism." When I tire of all

the "politics of dollarism," when I tire of speaking White, I seek refuge in poesy, in Gérald Godin, whose poesy of inclusion articulated in "Tango de Montréal" defeats dollarism.

## Why do you write?

I write "to encounter for the millionth time the reality of experience and to forge in the smithy of my soul the uncreated conscience of my race" [James Joyce]. I write to tell the Truth and shame the Somali Darod Devil. I write primarily to piss off Somalis. I write so I can "talk dirty and influence people" [Lenny Bruce]. I write to drive silly Billy hillbilly ignorant-arrogant Somalis bananas: "What is freedom of expression? Without the freedom to offend, it ceases to exist," Salman Rushdie said. Why bother to write if I can't offend?

  I write out of what Orwell called "aesthetic enthusiasm," out of the sheer pleasure of making a beautiful noise unto the Lord. I write out of "historical impulse": to see things as they are. I write to set the historical record straight. I write with political purpose, "out of the desire to push the world in a certain direction," as Orwell said. I write to fight the good fight of Faith, to stay the course, to finish my course, to keep the faith. I write to convince Somalis to kiss the clit, not to cut it off, not to mutilate it, not to murder it. I write just like Dylan Thomas: to make my statements on the way to my grave knowing that I "wrestle not against flesh and blood / but against principalities, against powers, against the rulers of the darkness of this world, against spiritual wickedness in high places," against Uncle Sam, against his boy-toy, against his *Kalab*, against his catamite, against Hassan Holo. I write blessed in Beulah, basking in Metanoia. If I don't write how else can I say "Togane is here"?

I write because I am most animated, most alive when I am writing. I write, I will write, I will keep on writing till falsehood flees, till bullshit perishes, till "Mercy and Truth meet together" in Mogadishu, "till Righteousness and Peace kiss each other" in Kissmaayo, till "the mountains and the hills break into songs of joy and all the trees clap their hands" [Isaiah 55:12]. I will keep on "battering the gates of heaven with storms of my prayers," till Allah flings open the gates of Heaven, my home. I write out of the sheer need to bear witness, to speak Truth to tyrants, to shout like that little brave boy: Mom, le roi est nu / Mom, Uncle Sam is now the buck-naked emperor. I write because Allah himself is in love with what I write; or as Blake put it, " Eternity is in love with the productions of time."

I write because my mom celebrated me, because I smattered in missionary's language, because my mom sang, "All those who used to pen books are in panic now / because of my champ / of my Bosteye," the champ who put chumps in their place. I write to make it impossible for Nuruddin Farah, for that Darod, Ogaden Ogre, to ever be able to brag, to brag again, "I am the only writer in the Somali nation. I am the only writer in my race of bullshitters!"

## Who is your audience?

My audience is my home audience, the Somalis: the hardest people to please in the world. If the Somalis are pleased with what I write, I can call a holiday, I can declare a holiday. I can go to dinner with the Lord for my job is done, for then the whole world is pleased. For, I repeat, the hardest people to please are Somalis who don't have "thank you" in their language, who are such ingrates that all they can say, all they can manage after I have done my damnedest and then some is, "Is that all?"

## Do you think there is an audience, outside of friends or other poets, for poetry?

Absolutely! I write with the whole world in mind, expecting the whole universe to pay attention. And as Willy Loman said, "Attention must be paid!" And I have been proven right. My poem "Arfaye" [in *Bridges: Literatures across Cultures*] is now studied in schools all over the world.

## Does your day job impact on your writing?

My friend, let's talk of poetry, the hardest job in the world. The muse does not, will not, cannot, dare not give you a chance to do anything else unless you just want to amuse yourself. "A line," said Yeats, "will take us hours maybe, yet if it does not seem a moment's thought our stitching and unstitching has been naught. ... For to articulate sweet sounds together is to work harder than all these and yet be thought an idler by the noisy set of bankers, schoolmasters, and clergymen..." Yes, that is why I can't hold onto a job, that is why I never let a job hold me down. I am busy; I am too busy 24/7 fucking the muse. Faulkner hit the nail on the head when he said: "One of the saddest things is that the only thing that a man can do for eight hours a day, day after day, is work. You can't eat eight hours a day, nor drink for eight hours a day, nor make love for eight hours – all you can do for eight hours is work, which is the reason why man makes himself and everybody else so miserable and unhappy." That is why I love to "lean and loaf at my ease observing / a spear of summer grass," as Whitman sang.

I am like the lilies of the field: "Behold how we grow, we toil not, neither do we spin. And yet I say unto you that even Solomon in all his glory was not arrayed like one of [us]." I am like that "Ol' Man River / that Ol' Man River / He don't say nothin' / but he must know somethin' / He just keeps rollin' / he keeps on rollin' along" from *Showboat*. Just like that Ol' Man River, I like to keep on rollin' along writing. As Frost articulated so succinctly, "My object in living is to unite / My avocation and my vocation / As my two eyes make one in sight."

## How many drafts do you usually go through before you are satisfied with a poem?

Like Paul Valery, I believe a poem is "never finished, only abandoned."

## Do you write with the intention of "growing a manuscript" or do you work on individual poems that are later collected into a book?

First, I name the book. The rest is easy to nail. I either threaten "to open a vein and watch myself bleed to death" or I persuade myself to, in the words of Gore Vidal, "Write something, even if it's just a suicide note." I call the book by its name till I am blue in the face. I keep hollering at it till I am hoarse. I keep calling it sweet names, whispering sweet nothings in its inner ear till it relents, till it responds by suddenly, miraculously, appearing as dictated by the Holy Spook!

## What is the toughest part of writing for you?

(a) Getting started (b) Knowing when it is truly finished! (c) Indulging in the bother and pleasure of publishing.

## What is your idea of a muse?

How about an advance of ten million bucks in my Swiss bank account and forcing me to be marooned on a deserted island?

## Do you have a favourite time and place to write?

My favourite time is dawn, in the kitchen, before the spoons and forks begin to wake up and fuss and fight, before the dishes dish it out to the spoons.

## Do you like to travel? Is travel important to your writing?

When I was young and foolish I traveled. Now that I am old and wise I travel all over the world without leaving my writing room, where I confront what Thomas Browne called "all Africa and her prodigies." To write, I have to stay put and stare at nothing until something shows up. Silent, sitting in quietude, in solitude, in an attitude of gratitude, in tune with myself, with infinity, cultivating eternity, "striving to learn before I die, what I am running away from and to and why?" as James Thurber advised. ∎

### Notes

Hawiye, Idoar, Abgal: different Somali clans

Darod: one of the most dominant clans in Somalia

Kalab: dog

Hassan Holo: current kakistocrat & kleptocrat wannabe tyrant of Somalia; Holo, spelled with only one "l" means beast in Somali

Mighty Mouth: Alias Mohamed Siad Barre, the Darod Dictator of Somalia: from 1969 to 1991

Kissmaayo: coastal city in Somalia

Nuruddin Farah: a very famous Somali novelist

Ogaden Og: a sub-clan of the Darod

MAHAMUD SIAD TOGANE

## That Time of Year

*That time of year thou mayst in me behold*
*When yellow leaves, or none, or few, do hang*
*Upon those boughs.*
         – Shakespeare's Sonnet 73

*Canada is a country in which for six months the trees go naked;*
*for the other six the people go naked.*
         – Somali bushwoman's definition of Canada in a BBC interview

It is that time of year here now when the maple trees go crazy with cold
And throw away their silken sarongs like silly-billy Somali bedlamites
When the creeping chilling airs of Fall render the sun's hot hard-on cold old
As bootless as Hugh Hefner's bloated with Viagra or as castrated catamite's
When bears hide hibernating dreaming of golden honey dandy days
When the sensible Canadian geese gong-honk their way way down South
Where the sun sizzles with savage Somali Summer endless hotdog dog days
When I feel the cold freezing creeping creepy carpet of winter death
Stealing on torturing on the green golden glad glades and dales of the forest
When Nature the Primary Scripture of Allah memento mories heedless humanity
When leaves proudly bust out "look ma no counterfeit color!" and put on their
   Sunday best
Only to fall fluttering into death's patient greedy cold captivity
Then do I remember
What a wonderful abbreviated Technicolor lie is this feverish lusty life's ember.

MAHAMUD SIAD TOGANE

# Susan Gillis

Photo: Alexandra Pasian

**Susan Gillis has lived on the Atlantic and Pacific coasts of Canada, and now lives most of the year in Montreal, where she teaches English at John Abbott College. Her books include *The Rapids* (Brick, 2012), *Volta* (Signature Editions, 2002), which won the A. M. Klein Prize for Poetry, and *Swimming Among the Ruins* (Signature Editions, 2000), and a chapbook, *Twenty Views of the Lachine Rapids* (Gaspereau Press, 2012). *Whisk*, with Yoko's Dogs, was published in 2013 by Pedlar Press.**

***Poetry Quebec:* You aren't native to Quebec. Where are you originally from?**

*Susan Gillis:* I grew up in Halifax, moved to the west coast in my late teens to go to school – and to follow Rilke's directive in Archaic Torso of Apollo: "you must change your life." I came to Montreal years later for the same reasons.

**How did Montreal change your life?**

The work I do for money. I don't know that I'd be teaching literature and creative writing to teenagers anywhere else in Canada. I'm not sure what I'd be doing instead; what I left was quite different, and I was ready to leave it, so there's no real chance I'd be running a vintage clothing store here – or any kind of business, for that matter. It has also partly shaped my subject matter and work habits. I miss the ocean, the tides, the daily routine of getting close to the edge of the solid earth, walking along the tide line, the smells, the sounds… I had to find someplace around Montreal I could get to easily that would stir me and settle me in similar ways. Urban pocket gardens weren't doing it, lovely and entrancing as they are. And city parks, well, they're city parks. It took a while, but eventually I found the Lachine Rapids, where there is a wonderful city park and also a bird sanctuary and the wilderness that is the river. That place has had a profound effect on my work. I can't walk to them mornings with a thermos of coffee, the way I used to walk out to the point in Victoria before settling in to a morning of writing, but still. They're always there. So I write in bed, in front of the long windows looking over rooftops and empty lots, and go to the rapids when I can. I also discovered I love winter! As long as it's sunny. Winter figures in a lot of my recent work.

## How did you first become interested in poetry?

I count a number of firsts, if that's allowed; the poetry of childhood, of teenage angst, of young adult optimism, of invention and reinvention, of... etc. But each time, at least as far as I remember, it was through hearing: the hearing of something jolted the explorer-me awake.

## What is your working definition of a poem?

I'm going to focus on the "working" part of this question, and consider it in terms of my own work rather than my reading of other poets. I suppose I am ready to call the stuff gathering in my notebook, or head, or wherever, a "poem" when its language charges up – when it acquires a cohering or loud or persisting sort of verbal energy, the ·specific qualities of which I can't define in a singular consistent way, since it's different each time. If I type up my notes before they gather this energy, they usually fizzle, or dead-end, or otherwise just give out. Once I take a piece to the computer and give it a file name, I'm ready to call it a poem, however unfinished it is. (Then I'll revise, both in the electronic file and on the paper copies, which can get terribly confusing, so I've developed a little system for that, but that's not part of this question.) So, a working definition of a poem? Stuff I type because it won't stay put in the notebook anymore.

## Describe your writing ritual.

I write in the mornings – at least, I start then. If I don't get started pretty much first thing, I tend not to be able to get started in a focused way all day. That said, I sometimes putter around, moving sort of sideways around writing, until the poem arrives and I go to my notebook. I find a routine helpful as long as it's flexible – sometimes breaking the routine creates good writing space.

## What is your approach to the writing of poems: inspiration-driven, structural, social, thematic...?

I've probably approached poetry in all these ways. Often I find the urge to speak comes from a combination of factors: sounds I've heard take shape in words that emerge from things I'd been thinking about... I don't often set out to write "about" a particular event or observation, but it will turn up in a poem eventually. Sometimes I want to investigate an idea I've encountered in my reading or in art or conversation – it could be anywhere – and I'll work it out in a language and situation that may or may not become a poem. Just last week I was struck by the way Princess Marya goes to the window in *War and Peace* after her father's funeral. I wanted to write about that, about her going to the window, so I did. Has it become a poem? Not sure yet.

## You're part of Yoko's Dogs, a renga writing group. Why renga, and how has being in this group invigorated or impacted on your writing?

Back in 2006 when I first floated this idea with Mary [di Michele], Jan [Conn] and Jane [Munro], I'd been working to develop the discipline of looking at the physical world. Not just looking of course, but mostly that. As a poet I wanted to get out of my head, in a sense, and find my subject matter in the world around me. I wanted to find ways to write about our physical, material world and the way we

SUSAN GILLIS

live in it that reflect the fact that those things matter. So I was exploring the traditions of nature poetry, especially Japanese and Chinese, and finding within their conventions an enormous sense of inter-relatedness between the natural and the human.

The ideas I found there of effacing the speaking self, letting go of authorship, removing the perceiving self from the surface of the poem – these were extremely attractive to me.

At the same time, renga collaborations were and are very much about authorship, particularly about the sensitive, attentive handling of somebody else's verse offering and the "whole cloth" of the poem as it grows. That was also exciting. I'd participated very casually in renga party games years before, and had a feeling it might be worth a more disciplined exploration.

Over the years of our practice I've learned a great deal about paring an image to its essence, about setting things in proximity, about excavating the unexpected in any given scene, and moving a poem into surprising territory. Collaboration is demanding, as you know, in what it asks us to yield, and yield to, and to make space for. And it's joyful in that it's a constant unfolding: I offer, say, a piece of pie and stand aside while the next person does something with it; someone offers me a silk tie and I get to decide what part of it to use. In collaboration you give up control of outcomes, which is very healthy.

**Do you write about Quebec?**
I have, in a sense, in that I've written about Habitat 67, Moshe Safdie's fabulous experiment on the bank of the river, and I've written a fair bit about the river

itself, particularly the Lachine Rapids. The poems aren't so much "about" these things as located on or in them. These days I'm working with specific sites on Montreal Island: my neighbourhood in Pointe-St-Charles, Sherbrooke Street, the old villages along the lakeshore... so much resonates from and in these places; they're very alive.

**Do you consider writing in English in Quebec a political act?**
*Living* in English in Quebec is a political act.

**Following your logic, if living in English here is a political act, then so must writing be. Would you agree?**
History and culture are living continuities. Writing and working and living in a minority language create an active engagement with those living continuities, a kind of claim-staking: Look, here's my little corner of history and culture, alive and well and kicking. Not threatening, just being. I suppose for some Quebec nationalists, any other culture's activity is threatening? Or the very notion of "just being" is false? I don't see my work or myself that way, but that doesn't mean others might not. Maybe not surprisingly, I have a strong distaste for Quebec politics.

As we speak, in the spring of 2013, I see a political Quebec challenging these aspects of its own continuity, through repressive language policies and legislation. The more pressure the Parti Québécois government (and/or Quebec nationalist interests working behind the scenes) applies to limitations on people's freedoms – the narrower they make those channels of history and culture – the more important, urgent and meaningful our work in

SUSAN GILLIS

English and all other languages becomes. (You can see I favour openness and equality in my politics! Always a losing proposition, I'm afraid.)

I'm hopeful that this anti-"other" fervour may be a passing form of hyperactivity, that most people in Quebec, whatever their cultural and national attachments, will object to having their world made smaller in these ways. I tend to agree with speculation that the PQ has been attempting to whip up separatist sentiment yet again, for its own political interests. And that the media select the most absurd examples of language policing, well aware of the effects on publicity and therefore money.

But you know, plenty of people throughout history have lived and continue to live with unbelievably restrictive political and social conditions. The present situation in Quebec is minor, in the big picture. And already it's beginning to abate, at least from the daily news. Much more pressing than the language issue is the problem of crumbling infrastructure in our cities.

### Why do you write?

Because I can't not. I've tried. It's harder than quitting smoking, which is hard, but do-able.

I don't mean to be facile with this question, but it seems so tied up with how I exist in the world. It's how I understand things.

### How many drafts do you usually go through before you are satisfied with a poem?

That depends on the poem. Usually quite a few, in several different stages. Generally I do a lot of writing around an idea before I begin thinking of it as a poem. Once it resolves, becomes clearer

and more cohesive, I type and print it. The drafts that follow the first typescript usually consist of fairly minor changes, not large structural or conceptual shifts. Though that happens too – particularly with poems I've let sit for a while, that I feel are underdeveloped. I love doing those major revisions – it's so satisfying.

### Do you write with the intention of "growing a manuscript" or do you work on individual poems that are later collected into a book?

After I "finish" a book, when I'm at the beginning of something again, I don't usually have a clear sense of what I'm really writing about. I find it useful then to choose a subject to explore. But soon that subject becomes more like a trap than an avenue. Then I shift modes: the process becomes one of just working on poems and seeing where they go, if they go – that's disorienting and disquieting, and often quite uncomfortable. The feeling that I have no idea what I'm doing or why can be very challenging, but it seems necessary to go all the way through it.

### Do you have a favourite time and place to write?

I'm not too tied to particulars in that regard, but generally mornings.

### Do you like to travel? Does it feed your writing in any way?

Yes. I love it, especially travelling in places I haven't been before. For lots of (mostly practical) reasons, I'm reluctant to travel as much as I used to. But it has been and continues to be very important, in its power to disrupt and disturb assumptions. I have two homes – the place I live during the school year and the place I live during the breaks, and

SUSAN GILLIS

having these two places means I'm never completely settled. So some of the valuable disruptive aspect of travel is always present in my life, and the valuable stability of home is also there.

**Do you think there is an audience, outside of friends or other poets, for poetry?**

Yes, a small one.

**Does your day job teaching at John Abbott College impact on your writing?**

Yes, by affecting my mental and emotional resources. It's mixed: as a teacher, I'm sharing and discovering with students. That's inspiring. But evaluating their work creates shrinkage in my brain. That's not inspiring. It's exhausting. My challenge is to spread my energy in a balanced way.

**What are the main challenges in teaching the understanding and appreciation of poetry?**

Oh, convincing students to stop worrying about whether they "get it" or not, and helping them to unearth, in themselves, other ways of engaging with what's in front of them than rational problem-solving. I have to get that right in the first few classes if we have any chance of going somewhere together during the term. There's a surprising (to me) lack of general knowledge, like that a weeping willow is a type of tree – that's a problem in understanding and appreciating poetry (never mind the lack of knowledge of art, history, literature, almost anything other than popular culture). I can't solve that in a semester. Apart from that, I would say that the challenges I face in teaching poetry are related more to the age and stage of life of my (teenage) students than to anything else. You can only go so far, you know, enticing people down the path; they have to come out to meet you. ■

*From Early Draft to Final Poem*

Here's a draft followed by the poem it became. The first two stanzas (not included here) turn out to be wind-up, though I still enjoy them. The third stanza (the first as reproduced here) is a mash-up of something else I was working on at the time; I'm not sure now why I thought it might spur me on here. It feels very much like an aside, like circling around, dumping fuel maybe so I could land? Anyway, the last stanza eventually became "Spring Storm," one of the anchoring poems in the series about the Lachine Rapids, published by Gaspereau in the chapbook *Twenty Views of the Lachine Rapids* and later collected in *The Rapids*, published by Brick. – SG

## The Body Runs Itself but Not on Air Alone

[...]

Sailors sometimes tell of being
plucked from the centre of a gale,
waking later somewhere safe
with no recollection of passage; a miracle.
But what name do we give the force
that propels us *into* the storm?
I had been tending the ~~garden fire~~ garden at home
when the sky split and a fierce gust
picked me up by the scruff of my neck
and threw me onto the road.
All parts of my life collapsed
like a collapsing city. Breathless ~~I was,~~
with a ~~stick~~ name in my throat, croaking
~~a name~~ it over and over, scratching it
into my skin. That was the first time.

SUSAN GILLIS

Yesterday I burned the toast
so I went down to the rapids.
It was not a bright morning.
Small rain pearled the windows
of the bus. The driver kept turning
the wipers off and on. Apart
from a man following a dog I was
alone, contemplating the river.
Close to shore a small twig
spun on an eddy. The eddy
was frilled like a doily, and seethed.
The twig was helpless to go anywhere
except around and around.
On the horizon plumes of smoke
rose like poplar trees. There was
the sun, punched into the sky
like the sky's navel. The river,
pricked and lifted by windhooks.
Mist puffing up, the sky black then white.
Columns of air I could have walked
like pathways to waiting jets,
walked into the skyhold. I'm telling you:
then the river reared up like a dragon,
scales flapping, the sun, smoke,
the small faint islands, all
collapsed in the froth of its lashing.
I had never been so small,
atomic. I was tossed. I have to
say "maelstrom." I wanted out.
I wanted time to turn back.
When I felt the ground again I was
shaking. It seemed I could reach
in any direction and touch the opposite
shore, the islands, the mist and smoke.
The gaps among things had closed.
I'm telling you this because I have not
been able to separate them, and now
all wounds are nothing, are blips,
leaf-loss. Nothing resists.
Know this: when I leave, I will not be gone.

## Spring Storm

Yesterday I burned the toast
so I went down to the rapids.
It was not a bright morning.
Close to shore a small twig
spun on an eddy. The eddy
was frilled like a doily, and seethed.
The twig was helpless to go anywhere
except around and around.
On the horizon plumes of smoke
rose like poplar trees. There was
the sun, punched into the sky
like the sky's navel. The river,
pricked and lifted by windhooks.
Mist puffing up, the sky black then white.
Columns of air I could have walked
like pathways to waiting jets,
walked into the skyhold. I'm telling you:
then the river reared up like a dragon,
scales flapping, the sun, smoke,
the far faint islands, all
collapsed in the froth of its lashing.
I had never been so small,
atomic. I was tossed. I have to
say "maelstrom." I wanted out.
I wanted time to turn back.
When I felt the ground again I was
shaking. It seemed I could reach
in any direction and touch the opposite
shore, the islands, the mist and smoke.
The gaps among things had closed.
I'm telling you this because I have not
been able to separate them, and now
all wounds are nothing, are blips,
leaf-loss. Nothing resists.
When I leave, understand, I will not be gone.

# Brian Campbell

Photo: Jacques Bernier

**Montreal-based poet, singer-songwriter, editor, and translator Brian Campbell is the author of *Passenger Flight* (2009), *Guatemala and Other Poems* (1994) and *Undressing the Night* (2007), a translation of the selected poems of Nicaraguan-Canadian poet Francisco Santos. His poetry, reviews, and essays have appeared in literary magazines such as *The Antigonish Review, Vallum, CV2, The New Quarterly, Grain, Prairie Fire, The Rover, Montreal Review of Books* and *The Saranac Review*. A finalist for the 2006 CBC Literary Award for Poetry, he received a Canada Council creative writing grant in 2011 towards the completion of his third collection of poetry. His independent music CD, *The Courtier's Manuscript*, was released in 2002. Brian Campbell teaches English as a Second Language to adults, and does freelance translation.**

**Poetry Quebec: Where are you originally from?**

*Brian Campbell:* I like to tell my adult ESL students – mostly immigrants – that I too am an immigrant, from an exotic place called Ontario. That I had to show my passport, change my money at the border, even learn a new language. No, seriously, I came here from my native Toronto in the early '90s at the biblical age of thirty-three. And I did have to suffer a kind of death – not a crucifixion, but a kind of death – in order to live the happy kind of life I have now.

**Why did you come to Quebec?**

I could go on and on. To find inspiration. To test a relationship that I did not find entirely inspiring. (The relationship failed the test, mainly because I wanted it to.) Because I was excited by French culture, fashion and architecture. By the seeming superabundance of stunning, stylish, vivacious women. Because I was sick of my native city, which seemed – and is – very much a wasteland. Because I was dried up creatively, and tired of conversations with fellow poets who would always wind up complaining about that corporate, commercial, soulless, pulseless T.O. Because going to Montreal seemed like going to another country – it is the most European metropolis in North America – without severing my connection to friends and family just down the highway from here. Because it was affordable to live here, and work part-time to support my writing and music, which I have done since, something that would be pretty well impossible where I came from. Because it was convenient to take a teacher's degree here. At that point in my life, becoming an expatriate – in a place like Madrid, Tokyo or Buenos Aires – seemed the only other option available.

### When did you encounter your first Quebec poem?

My reflexive answer is the song "Suzanne" by Leonard Cohen. That was in grade 7. Teaching songs as poetry or "poetry put to music" was new then, in the early '70s, and this song was relatively new. I appreciate the enlightened English teacher – an elderly British man – who played it on the little record player in front of the classroom. The poem – or song – is very Montreal, isn't it? When I first went to the Vieux Port, there she was – Our Lady of the Harbour. It's a very bohemian, romantic piece, and may have planted the seeds for my attraction to this city.

### When and how did you first become interested in poetry?

When I wrote my first poem, at the age of sixteen. Oddly enough, this too was in a classroom. A substitute English teacher had us do a poem based on the famous William Carlos Williams poem about eating the plums in the refrigerator. The product of that exercise I still consider worthwhile; it later got published in a university magazine.

But the North York suburb that I grew up in was not a very auspicious place to cultivate an interest in poetry or become a poet. Hardly anyone there even read a book! I didn't find a proper sense of community or environment until I went to University of Toronto. There I did an undergraduate degree in English – mostly poetry courses – and fell under the sway of T.S. Eliot, Yeats, Dylan Thomas, Ted Hughes, Sylvia Plath, and others. Then I started to build a body of my own work, and consider poetry a primary interest.

### What is your working definition of a poem?

A poem is an instance of concentrated, rhythmic language that strikes us with a revelation of what it is to be alive.

### Is this something you came to as a result of having written a particular sort of poem or body of poems, or did you first begin writing poetry with this in mind?

I actually came up with this while preparing to teach a class through the Quebec Writers' Federation "Writers-in-CEGEPs" program. I asked myself questions that I eventually would pose to the students: What is poetry to you? What ideas come to mind when you hear the word poetry? (The students said things like "poetry rhymes" or "poetry is beautiful language" – both true, as far as they go.) I compiled a number of "definitions" that became a hand-out entitled, tellingly, "Poetry – some definitions of the indefinable." These included Marianne Moore's "imaginary gardens with real toads in them" and Emily Dickinson's famous remark that "If I read a book and... feel physically as if the top of my head were taken off, I know that is poetry." Then I thought hard and came up

BRIAN CAMPBELL

with my own functional definition that reflects, to some degree, the priorities of my own practice: distillation and musicality of language, the unusual rather than clichéd.

Of course, I wouldn't allow myself to be hobbled by that or any other encapsulation. Poetry and prose exist on a continuum; at times in a given piece they work well together. I also think of what Margaret Atwood once said: "Poetry isn't written from the idea down. It's written from the phrase, line and stanza up, which is different from what your teacher taught you to do in school."

### Do you have a writing ritual?

I'm a rather impulsive writer who goes through cycles of productivity and non-productivity. But I do have an ideal ritual: get up in the morning, have the day relatively free before me, brew a good coffee and sit down and create. I try to arrange my circumstances to allow that ritual to happen. When I manage to actually do it, that's when I'm usually at my happiest.

### What is your approach to the writing of poems?

In my twenties and thirties I was very inspiration driven, which meant, of course, that as I became more self-critical, my production became very sporadic, and eventually – shortly after I arrived here – shut down altogether. This, of course, was very distressing. Eventually, I discovered a songwriting voice; I wrote about sixty songs over a space of ten years – even went so far as to recording an album – before going back to poetry. Right now I find that I can open up my laptop and let the words come, and I can often shape them into something that surprises me, something quite good.

Some poems are riffs on language; others are spurred by reading or experience, and a few have been driven by a need to deal with a certain theme.

### Earlier you said that one of the reasons you left Toronto was because you were dried up creatively, and now you say the same thing happened once you arrived in Montreal. How do you explain that? What do you think brought out the songwriting voice in you?

You make me think of Cavafy's famous poem, "The City." But things weren't quite as bad as that. Although I enjoyed and was intrigued by Montreal, it took some time to get an authentic feel for it. I felt I had to learn the French language, to integrate with the social realities here, so that my expression vis-à-vis this place would be natural, or at least, second nature.

At the risk of sounding trite, Montreal is a romantic place: the life of couples is more primary here than in the city where I'm originally from. Songwriting came out of solitude and longing – nearly all the songs are love songs or songs of loneliness, although there are also some social justice and humorous pieces. It also came out of a level of mastery of the guitar that I reached here, and some happy discoveries – mainly, coalescences between certain chord progressions and the lyrics they evoked – that first took place in a certain walk-up apartment on rue Brébeuf in the Plateau.

### Do you think that being part of the English-speaking minority in Quebec influences your writing?

Quebec is a province of minorities, and the most beleaguered minority is the so-called majority, les francophones. Being

BRIAN CAMPBELL

surrounded by French, and speaking it every day – I lived on the Plateau for eight years before moving to the more multicultural Mile End – means I've absorbed French vocabulary and expressions, and these can inform and influence the words I choose in English. I have a number of poems that bring French phrases and sensibilities into English; these include my prose poems, which follow, after all, what was originally a French form.

## Do you think that writing in English in Quebec is a political act?

This strikes me as a tiresome question; it seems to hark back to the early years of language legislation, or at least when Lucien Bouchard was in power. Generally speaking, I support that legislation, despite some of its absurd implications – sign measuring and the like. (Recently, under the current Marois government, old hackles have been raised by the Office Québécois de la langue française ordering an Italian restauranteur to replace Italian words, including *pasta*, in his menus with their French equivalents – but it is notable that this and a few other similar excesses led to the resignation of the head of that agency.) Bill 14, an expansion of language legislation under consideration by the minority PQ government as I write, has led to ominous headlines in the English press. But, in its rough-and-all-too-unready-way, the Charter of the French Language has worked in terms of preserving this French corner in an otherwise English-dominated North America.

Of course, I chose to come here after the Charter was in place and its effects were already apparent. There was no ques-

tion to me about learning the language of the majority, and I'm sure I would do the same if I moved to any other place. A language is a richness, a blessing, an alternative way of seeing things. The only reason I write in English is that it is the language I dream in, that I've mastered.

## Why do you write?

Primarily, for the joy of it – there is almost no greater pleasure than the rush of creating a good poem. All the aesthetic decisions involved in drafting and honing can be a great pleasure as well. I love the music of language, and poetry, it seems, is what I'm best at. I also write because through this form of expression, I learn even for myself what I am thinking and feeling. My best work comes as a surprise: if it fails to surprise me, I'd say that's a strong indication that it fails as poetry.

## Does your day job impact on your writing?

Actually, for the most part my day job is an evening job. Teaching English as an Additional Language is in some ways a stimulus; relating to it through my students makes me relate to it again as new, in all its eccentricities. It's also a very social job, a nice break from the solitude of writing. Insofar as I have to be on call for supply work during the day, and open to other things like translation contracts to supplement that income, my routine can be turned upside down, and it can be hard to get back into a creative rhythm.

## How many drafts do you usually go through before you are satisfied with a poem?

I now write and revise with my laptop, so what constitutes a draft has changed somewhat from way back when, in the typewriter era. I'm quite confident now of my cuttings, pastings, and deletions, but when I start to feel unsure the changes I'm making are improvements, I copy and paste the whole poem within the same file and continue shaping the pasted version. After I've reached a point where the poem feels done, I print out all drafts, and then delete all but the most recent draft. I keep all the hard copies of my so-called drafts. It's rare, but it has happened that I've gone back to a draft and found it better than a revised version. Most of the time, I go through about six or seven "cut and paste" drafts, although the majority of changes that have taken place in these early drafts have disappeared into the ether. Then on the printouts I make handwritten changes, fine tunings, which lead to new printouts. There could be as many as twenty of these – or as few as one or two.

## Do you have a favourite time and place to write?

Right now, most of my creative writing I do in the morning, right after I've woken up with a cup of coffee. This, at the kitchen table, a pleasant, sunlit place with lots of plants and art on the walls. I also like to write in cafés. Blogging, revising, and other writing-related work I'm likely do at any time, anywhere, but often late at night or in the wee hours of the morning – in my home office.

## Do you write with the intention of "growing a manuscript" or do you work on individual poems that are later collected into a book?

Mostly I have done the latter. With *Passenger Flight*, after writing about twenty prose poems, I got the idea of writing a book of them, and then deliberately wrote in that form until I had enough to put together a book. This was

a new experience for me; it may never be repeated.

## What makes a "prose poem" – an oxymoron if there ever was one – a poem?

Fellow Montreal poet Maxianne Berger wrote a nice comment on *Passenger Flight* that unfortunately didn't make it to the back of my book, but is on Signature's website: "Brian Campbell uses every device available within the poet's armamentarium – except the line break. This allows Campbell's somewhat eccentric persona to speak with manic breathlessness as his 'one open eye' explores the 'flexuous' possibilities of the imagination. The mind fills a void. It does fill. Have faith."

I love that word, armamentarium. Makes me think at once, for some reason, of both armadillos and of medieval coats of armour. As well as of course the abstract but etymologically more closely related word, armaments. Her comment says a lot about that hybrid form, the prose poem. Yes, in a number of the prose poems, we have rhymes, rhythms, alliterations, repetitions – the very stock and stuff of poetry. And yet to the extent that prose poems are not constrained by line or stanza break, they can seem wild, slapdash – "manic" and "breathless" as she says – or fall into realms of anecdote, joke, absurdity. At other times they can express a loose, jazzy but very pure music. Prose poems can remind us that so-called free verse is really not so free.

## What is the toughest part of writing for you?

Making the switch after the long, intensive period of editing – putting together a book manuscript, say – back to raw creativity. Someone said – I don't know who – that you write loose but edit tight. Writing and editing are definitely very different activities that seem to draw on different regions of the brain. After obsessively scrutinizing every word before it goes to print, it's hard to put those reflexes aside in order to enter into the unmediated, to generate something new. Sometimes, it requires a long fallow period.

## What is your idea of a muse?

She's a nearly impossible combination: caring, daring, and beautiful. She's young, wise as the ages, loves the poet's poetry, inspires it constantly, and is never ever banal. She makes love with total abandon, then disappears into mists so that in anguished longing the poet composes the most magnificent love poems ever written, just to bring her back. And yet she is always there, somehow, supporting the poet's serene creation. In other words, she probably doesn't exist. Yeats had Maude Gonne; she came pretty close: was daring, beautiful, but almost utterly uncaring (it's hard to get even that basic combination right.) My own partner – we'll soon be married – is the closest approximation of a muse I've found in the so-called real world. Yes, I could say she is my muse.

## Is travel important to your writing?

Funny I should come to this question now: I'm doing this part of the interview in the same Quebec City bed and breakfast where I wrote "Casements," a prose poem in *Passenger Flight*. The night view out the window here – a spectacular view of the sparkling lights of the city – is much the same one that inspired that poem (actually, I'm in the room next door). I can see into other apartments across the narrow street here just outside the walls of the old city. It put me in mind of Baudelaire's "Les fenêtres" ("Windows") from *Paris Spleen* – I had brought Louise Varese's translation along for the ride, and bought the original French version at a bookstore around the corner and read it that afternoon. So I wrote a palimpsest of that poem.

The title poem of my first collection, *Guatemala and Other Poems*, I wrote a few years after a six-month trip to Mexico and Guatemala, where I learned Spanish, among other things. In *Passenger Flight*, travel, in all its glitziness and romantic expectation, is a major theme – as the title would suggest. In my forthcoming collection, I have a section called "Getaways"– poems inspired by hotels, cottages, resort towns here in Quebec. At times I still feel like a cultural tourist in this province I moved to more than twenty years ago. Yet for all that, I am not a frequent traveler. My own passport hasn't been renewed in years. But in as much as I engage in that most basic level of writing – writing spurred by immediate surroundings – travel can refresh and trigger creation.

## Do you have a favourite Quebec poet?

I don't have a favourite anything. I have a soft spot for Saint-Denys Garneau, the first Québécois poet I read in the original: poems like "Cage d'oiseau," "Accompaniment" and, of course, his journals are very immediate and touching. I've read some very impressive poems by Yves Préfontaine: "Peuple inhabité" is a kind of masterpiece. I very much enjoy Hélène Dorion and Louise Desjardins; indeed, I recently translated a lengthy poem by the latter of those

BRIAN CAMPBELL

two. In English, the first poets that spring to mind are Leonard Cohen and Irving Layton, two seminal influences I scarcely ever read now. Layton I hardly think of as a Quebec poet, although of course he was; a number of his strongest poems were written in, and about, Toronto, where he lived for many years; others in Greece and Italy. I think of him more as a Jewish-Canadian poet. Of course, I can't acclaim his whole oeuvre, but even his crap has a winning liveliness. Others in my "Quebec pantheon" include A.M. Klein, Artie Gold, Robyn Sarah, and Carmine Starnino.

**Do you think there is an audience, outside of friends or other poets, for poetry?**

Actually, "audience" – with its roots in the auditory and relation to words like "audition" and "auditorium" – connotes a throng of listeners, so it strikes me as a more suitable term for performance art, i.e. spoken word. The word has a very contemporary, crowd-pleasing feel; although I love doing poetry readings, I see who attends the typical reading – mostly other people who write or try to write poetry, family, friends – so that inclines me to answer no to your question. "Readership" is probably the more appropriate word for poetry, at least for the kind I write. If "audience" is taken to include readership, then the answer becomes obvious. In the long term, yes... and only for a tiny minority of poets and poems. Those who get anthologized, get on academic curricula and the like. Those who become part of the cultural heritage. If me and mine be among them, only time will tell. If time – or rather humanity – continues. Even that is very much in doubt. ∎

## The Stillness Minnow

I cup my hands, close them around it, slowly, slowly...trying to move my fingers without moving. It darts away.

We were closer to it when we lay together, sharing breaths and whispers. We were closerwhenwerestedinsilence,caressingourprivates,makingthemwarm,engorge.

Now I in chair, you in couch, books in hand, are clamshelled in fashion state-ments. And it suspends in the air between us.

Its scales are golden, with two bands of blue down its sides. Under transparent skin, a single, silver lung contracts, expands. The tiny glove of its heart beats. A luminous bubble comes from its mouth, floats up out of sight.

BRIAN CAMPBELL

## Mountain

We've placed a cross on your shoulder,
erected a transmission tower,
planted a spindly flag.

We've tunneled through you,
necklaced you with roads, paths,
apartments, mansions clutching
like pearls at your throat.

You, who pressed forth
forced by unrelenting magma,
who rose
earthen breast, back
primordial.

Now the city gathers round,
temples, spires
obeisant to your deep bass voice –
but freeways, office buildings, industrial parks
oblivious.

We live beside you in tiny flats
watch phantasmal screens,
eat, recline,
groom ourselves for the daily backandforth
squirm into leather
for nights in halogen town.

Still – certain hours – you block the sun:
chilled by your encroaching gloom,
we peer from windows, terraces, to see you
throw off our ropes and stays, to loom.

# Charlotte Hussey

Photo: Zoe Arniotis

**Charlotte Hussey teaches Old Irish and Arthurian Literature at Dawson College in Montreal. She has published *Rue Sainte Famille*, which was shortlisted for the QSPELL Awards, and a chapbook, *The Head Will Continue to Sing*. Writing her doctorate on the Modernist poet H.D. re-awakened Charlotte's love of antiquity and led to her latest collection, *Glossing the Spoils*.**

CHARLOTTE HUSSEY

*Poetry Quebec:* **Where are you originally from?**

*Charlotte Hussey:* I was born in Maine, a state that has a lot of Franco-Americans, many of whom speak a dialect similar to Québécois. During my childhood summers at Wells Beach, my playmates' Québécois grandmother cooked us the thinnest, butteriest, most delicious crêpes, my version of Proust's madeleines.

**Why did you come to Quebec?**

I moved to Montreal in 1974 after living too far away in San Francisco and feeling too overwhelmed by New York City. Montreal was a slightly more "European" version of Maine; it was nearly home and the crêpes rocked!

**When did you encounter your first Quebec poem?**

Arriving in Montreal, I enrolled in an English M.A. at Concordia University. My classmates were Laurence Hutchman, Brian Bartlett, and Anne Cimon. We started a writing group that Maxianne Berger soon joined. Their poems were my first encounter with Quebec poetry.

**How did you first become interested in poetry?**

Ending up in a Wheaton College undergraduate creative writing class by default. The anthropology and sociology classes were full, but my third choice – creative writing – wasn't. Moved by my backcountry Maine imagery and my erupting emotions, the professor coaxed forth my poems. I soon won all the school poetry prizes. I went on to interview Charles Olson in nearby Gloucester, Maine, and did my thesis on his *Projective Verse*. I remember driving Olson back from the bar where we met. Olson was at least six feet eight inches, a size suiting his sweeping manifestos and sprawling epics. It was a challenge to stuff this somewhat inebriated giant into my small TR-6.

## Do you see any Projective Verse influence in your own writing?

Olson certainly influenced my fledgling poems. I still love to sprawl poems across the page/"field," particularly ones about a marsh or the sea. Doing an M.F.A. in the late '80s, I discovered Curtis B. Brandford's *Yeats at Work,* a study of Yeats's draft revisions. Yeats was a rigorous reviser, early and late. Blown away by his vigorous, exacting craftsmanship, I wrote a critical paper about his metrical revisions. After that I started experimenting with sonnets, villanelles, and then the glosas comprising *Glossing the Spoils.*

Olson's use of dreams, mythology, history, and antiquity exerts a continuing influence. Olson's fascination with Mayan hieroglyphics and culture inspired me to study North American Native literature. Olson wrote his *Mayan Letters* in the '50s, urging his readers to renounce their European heritage and embrace Native New World Cultures. But an awakening occurred in 1981 when Anne Cameron published *Daughters of Copper Woman,* her retelling of stories entrusted to her by a secret society of Nootka women. A strident cultural appropriation debate flared up with Lee Maracle taking Cameron to task. Although the imagination is, in essence, a free agent, Canadian writers began to realize it is not morally correct to speak for those you have colonized and exploited.

Charles Simic in *"Dime-Store Alchemy"* writes that "America is a place that the Old World shipwrecked." As such, immigrants be they French, English, or other, have an uneasy relationship with, say, Quebec. Frankly, none of us are deeply rooted here, nor do we have ancient rituals and traditions connecting us to Quebec's animals, plants, and land, ones that could help us live more in harmony with nature. That said, when I went back "home" to England to do research for *Glossing the Spoils,* I was not from there either. UK writers can include Celtic or Anglo-Saxon pagan deities and otherworldly marvels in their poetry because they spring from the land itself. Bringing such references across the Atlantic is like washing up with bits of flotsam and jetsam salvaged from your sinking ship – not much to work with.

## Would you say that "Language Writing" is an extension of Projective verse?

I am far from an expert on L=A=N=G=U=A=G=E Poetry. I can offer some off-the-cuff comments. During his senior year in high school, Olson took third place in the National Oratorical Contest, and his poetry has a rhetorical drive and concern with big ideas rather than feelings, something I see in the meta-thinking and political critic embedded in certain Language Writing. Olson also defined a poem as a field of energy, energy that moved from poet to reader. Working with this energy concept, the early Language Writers redefined a poem's energies to flow in two directions: (1) back onto the poem to probe its artificiality; and (2) forward to question the reader's ability to interpret it.

## Do you consider what is being done by "Language" writers, especially here in Quebec, where "language" has political/cultural overtones, valid or relevant?

I have a visual, visceral sensibility that didn't draw me to the L=A=N=G=U=A=G=E Poetry movement. I guess, though, that a L=A=N=G=U=A=G=E poet's love of multiple meanings and playful puns would well suit a bilingual Quebec writer.

## What is your working definition of a poem?

Ideally, my poetry should dramatize a lyric epiphany. It should allow some larger wholeness to glimmer through, a wholeness with mythological reverberations. Yeats's notion of a poem as a visceral argument also influenced *Glossing the Spoils*. Each glosa, a form derived from Biblical glossing, argues against, questions, or talks back to four consecutive lines taken from an earlier text. It was exciting to write a glosa that conversed with, say, a 1,300-year-old text from a time when otherworldly marvels were common and works of art, like that of the Old Irish *Voyage of Bran, Son of Febal*, were instinctual, surreal, wild.

## Do you have a writing ritual?

I rely a lot on sleep thinking. I calmly read over a draft before sleep. It is like asking the unconscious for help in a light, playful way, rather than desperately demanding needed answers. Waking up, I record any remembered dream bits and then write in bed for a couple of hours.

## What is your approach to writing a poem?

It depends. With *Glossing the Spoils*, I undertook a march from the eighth-century, Old Irish *Voyage of Bran, Son of Febal* through to the fifteenth-century, Middle English *Le Morte d'Arthur* by Sir Thomas Malory. Fortunately as a Quebec poet, I found many texts written in Old or Norman French. Thus, the inspiration driving many of my glosas came from such Old French writers as Chretien de Troyes, Wace, Robert de Boron, and, of course, Anonymous.

A different inspiration drives my free verse. I simply fill up a dime-store journal, nugget out emotionally charged bits, arranged them in a poem skeleton, and build from there. I draw primarily on daily experiences and night dreams. My current work-in-progress is inspired by the supernatural border ballad, "Tam Lyn." I have collaged this ballad and then free-written off the collage imagery. Working with these layers, I am focusing on threshold experiences implicit in "Tam Lyn" that overlap those of my own life.

## Do you write with the intention of "growing a manuscript," or do you work on individual poems that are later collected into a book?

My intentions vary. *Rue Sainte Famille* was a collection of individual poems, resulting from journaling about everyday experiences, feelings, night dreams, etc. With *Glossing the Spoils*, I purposely marched through early Western European literature, aiming to write just twenty-eight glosas, a symbolic number for me.

The "Tam Lyn" project strikes a middle ground between spontaneity and intent. Using the ballad as a loose structural device, I can draft free verse poems of an undetermined number. Growing a manuscript with intent can be reassuring, taking the poet on an unfolding, heroic journey across numerous initiatory thresholds. But too much forward planning is deadly.

## How many drafts do you usually go through before you are satisfied with a poem?

Innumerable drafts. I do a lot of free writing off a poem skeleton to get "stuff" to feed back into it. The resulting rich chaos means courageously grabbing at unexpected creatures from the sea.

**What is the toughest part of writing for you?**

The toughest thing is to be more prolific and less perfectionistic. My perfectionism, coupled with the demands of supporting my family, has meant I haven't published enough. Much can be said for people who plunge in and go for quantity rather than quality.

**What positive effects, if any, has your day job had on your writing?**

My day jobs certainly have eaten away at my writing practice. After doing a Ph.D., I dropped out of the tenure-track stream to write, instead of staying to theorize about poetry. Nevertheless, academia honed my research skills, and without McGill University's world-class library, I would never have read all the Early and Medieval texts used in *Glossing the Spoils*. My McGill teaching job also provided free transportation to Northern Quebec native communities.

**Do you think that being part of the English-speaking minority in Quebec affects your writing?**

Possibly, but today one belongs to internet writing communities. Finding your niche shared by those living in Australia, the UK, or California means you are not confined to a Montreal anglophone ghetto. I have been more conscious of my minority status as a dancer, as I dance "in French." Dance is a way to keep up my French – albeit a French given over to body parts and choreographed moves.

Granted, living as a minority can precipitate an identity quest. The stimulus for my identity search was not Quebec's "two solitudes" but its third, found in Northern Cree communities. Teaching in Chisasibi, Eastmain, Waskaganish and Mistissini, I grew fond of the myths and folklore that breathed life into my students, in spite of their sadly waning, hunting culture. A student's thirteen-year-old son killed his first bear. That day, nobody came to class, celebrating, instead, his rite of passage. Its mingling of animal and human energies piqued my imagination. Still there was a pressure, culminating in white guilt attacks that stopped me from writing about the North as an outsider. In fact, a McGill colleague, nobler than me, gave up her promising writing career to fly all over the North helping the Cree turn their oral stories into Cree language teaching tools. This silenced her.

One day, a Cree student subtly sent me off in search of my own myths and tales. Nudged, acutely aware of the cultural appropriation debate, I flew to the UK and began researching the mythopoetic sources of Early Western Europe. This was not easy. Greek and Roman aesthetics and mythologies are still the common currency of Western literature. The surreal potency, for example, of the Celts has long been suppressed. My poem "Four Corners" addresses the repressive, palimpsest-like nature of literary history.

**Do you think that writing in English in Quebec is a political act?**

Writing is a political act: A writer must express her world view in a particular language against all the other culturally constructed languages. World views breed conflicts: In the late '80s, I had considered writing a long poem about my relative, Sarah Hanson, a fourteen-year-old girl taken into captivity in 1724 by the Mohawk and brought on foot from Dover, New Hampshire to Kanesatake, Quebec. The 1990 Oka Crisis, a land dispute between the Mohawk and the citizens of Oka, halted my research. Not knowing much about her captivity, I had polarized it as a Mohawk/English one. Recently, I was able to reframe it from a more workable French/English perspective, when I discovered that Sarah, age seventeen, was married to a young Frenchman, Captain Jean-Baptist Sabourin and that their settler's cabin is part of The Greenwood Centre in Hudson, Quebec.

Writing as a political act also manifested while doing my doctorate. I began seeing how facility in Classical Latin and Greek granted a poet higher status at conferences and in the literary world. (Anne Carson was on my doctoral committee!!) I began resisting this Classical hegemony. I took up the banner for Celtic mythology, a marginalized mythology not unlike that of the Cree or Mohawk, that gives pride of place to nature, its spirits, and to a dreamlike otherworld that parallels our own. Celtic mythology has given us the Arthurian Matters of Britain, with many of its continental texts written in Old German and Old French. This brought me full circle to Quebec where I am now attempting to read Jean D'Arras's "The Romance of the Faery Melusine" in Old French.

## Why do you write?

I write because I love crafting well-made things. I write to understand myself. I write to travel through threshold images into a deeper connection with the universe. Finally, I write to make daily meaning in an often meaningless world.

## Who is your audience?

My audience depends on what I am writing. *Glossing the Spoils* was written out of an inner need to explore my roots and with little market consideration. It got snapped up in the UK; people there love Western European mythopoetic stuff. I belong to some online communities – with worldwide reach – that read my poetry. My new manuscript has a Scottish folkloric base, but is set in North America's '60s and '70s. Hopefully, its audience will be more homegrown.

## Do you think there is an audience, outside of friends and other poets, for poetry?

Recently, too much has been made of the "death of poetry." Poetry has always been with us since the earliest recorded Sumerian prayers honouring their Anunnaki pantheon. Poetry persists because it is low maintenance – all you need is a reed pen and a clay tablet, a ballpoint and a sheet of paper. Poetry persists because it allows us to cry out about our human lot. More poetry is being written and published today than at any other time. This is not just a North American phenomenon. In the Middle East, Arabic poetry fuels political rallies, while their version of our "American Idol" is the widely televised poetry competition, "Million's Poet." Do we gripe about poetry's stagnation because a poet will never receive the salary of hockey player?

## What is your idea of a muse?

My love of native literature led me, at one point, to train in shamanism. All I can

CHARLOTTE HUSSEY

say is that muse figures – animal or otherwise – are there. You can liken them to the imaginary friends we played with as children, and who is more creative than a child? These helpers are there if artists can let down their guard. My doctoral thesis consisted of a correspondence between myself and the Imagist poet H.D. I wrote to her, sent her my poetry, and although dead, H.D. wrote back, or so I fruitfully imagined. I graduated with high honours.

## Is travel important to your writing?

Travelling is creatively stimulating. The photos and travel journal from a UK trip fed my glosas. But travelling via my imagination has been key! I've indulged in shamanic journeying, active imagining, daydreaming myself back into a photo, re-entering a night dream, and time travelling to an earlier historical period. This inner journeying has been the happy result of less than ideal circumstances: raising a child on a small income.

## Do you have a favourite Quebec poet?

There are a number of Quebec poets I admire such as Carolyn Marie Souaid, Endre Farkas, Julie Bruck, Susan Gillis, Mark Abley, Maxianne Berger, Anne Cimon and more. Nevertheless I want to point to what in Quebec is still largely overlooked – its native writers. I admire Cree poet Margaret Sam-Cromarty's verse for opening my senses and taking me deep into the subarctic bush with her hunter father. I am saddened by her laments over what the James Bay Hydro Project has inflicted upon her lands and people. And the Mohawk writer Peter Blue Cloud, whose "Coyote Did Not Want to Create People," reminds me, as a poet, to consider an earthy, don't-take-yourself-too-seriously approach.

## Do you write about Quebec?

My writing is grounded in my small yellow room, in a small brick house on avenue Royal in NDG – a place necessary, when time travelling, to leave from and return to. ∎

131

## Four Corners

*I am honored in praise.*
*Song is heard*
*in the Four-Cornered Fortress,*
*four its revolutions.*
                    – Preiddeu Annwn

Held with poets and plunderers
in this sea-surrounded keep,
I wander its deep halls, dirt floors
strewn with rushes and the herbs of the world,
under which are grease, bones, spittle.
In a niche nested in a wall, the glazed
leaves of a parchment buckle slightly,
as if come alive, to reveal
the raised letters of a phrase:
*I am honored in praise,*

a phrase burnished in heavenly gold
that overwrites some faded heresy
inked in cinnabar and cochineal;
the dried blood of an old grammar,
navigation or lament, injured
by a scraping hand. Deeper, more covered
are faces, grey, overgrown with lichens,
voices that can wake the hills,
cries, sounding birdlike, burred.
*Song is heard,*

sneaking up from ruination,
where she has crouched for so long;
little, wan woman, ringlets of hair,
fall like flax to her calloused heels.
As noon and jet mingle, her lath
body seems cut from a coppice.
She stretches a crooked palm, arm
*genius loci,* making new growth
break through the stones of this fastness,
*in the Four-Cornered Fortress.*

In an underground cell, a solitary
staff planted in the beaten earth
blossoms into a single stemmed tree;
she hums, bathing my spiraling ears
with tiny, rapid waves,
until the walls of this angular prison
open and, from all directions, bees or spirits
swarm my heart like a storied hive.
Amber tears flood its chambers. I listen,
*four its revolutions.*

133

# kaie kellough

kaie kellough is a Montreal word-sound systemizer. He is the author of two books of poetry: *lettricity* (Cumulus, 2004), and *maple leaf rag* (Arbeiter Ring, 2010), which was nominated for the Manuela Dias Design Award. kellough is the voice of two sound recordings, *vox:versus* (wow, 2011), a suite of conversations between voice and instrument, and *esion* (howl, 2013).

His print and sound work is underwritten by rhythm and by a desire to dis-and re-assemble language and meaning, and his art emerges where voice, language, music, and text intersect. He has performed and published internationally, and is presently working on a novel and on a series of language-based visual works.

### Poetry Quebec: Are you a native Quebecer?

*kaie kellough:* no, am not a native québ. was born in vancouver & grew up in calgary. i'm a western canadian who migrated east to montréal 14.5 yrs ago. i moved to montréal bcuz i wanted to be in a large, diverse arts-friendly urban center as far from calgary's conservatism, suburban sprawl & cowboy culture as i cd possibly get, tho i always enjoyed watching bull-riding. i am bilingual, & montréal is where my parents met, so i felt some conxion to the city. tho montréal is located in québec, i identify as montréalais more than as québécois. if i lived in toronto or vancouver i would feel a similar ambivalence toward the prov-

ince at large. i identify with the modern multicultural urban milieu, which does not exist throughout the province. as an urbanite my daily life has much more in common with a vancouverite's than with that of someone from hérouxville.

### How did you encounter your first Quebec poem?

don't know abt the first one, but know that the first one that reverberated in my cranium was am klein's "Heirloom" in *20th Century Poetry & Poetics* edited by gary geddes. but years before that i'd read *Jacob Two-Two Meets the Hooded Fang*, & so mordecai was the first montréal author i ever read.

### When did you first become interested in poetry?

i'd always been a reader & lover of language. in my late late teens i started reading some harlem renaissance cats (don't remember how i got turned on to them) like langston hughes & countee cullen. they stunned me bcuz they were writing about topics i'd never seen poets approach. hughes in particular was writing in a blues form, so the poetry was linked to a 20th-century african-american musical genre, it was anchored here, in the sound & culture of the multiracial americas & it therefore included me.

at some point i was introduced to the jamaican dub poets. when i was younger i was impressed by their rhythm, righteous social criticism & declamatory style. they were rebels, outsiders & self-proclaimed authorities, poetic pundits commenting on their society. but as i got older their volume & righteous posture lost some appeal. also, the dub message seemed to be caught in a retro-loop, repeating itself.

i was attracted to the beatniks for similarly youthful reasons. i dug that '50s be-bop hipster posture as it clashed with the brando rebel attitude, classic american. but today the only beats i still read are amiri baraka, bob kaufman & ginsberg (we share the same birthday, june 3rd). ginsberg led me directly to whitman, and from there i read on thru some of the major poets from the states, the caribbean, latin america. i came very late to canadian poetry, but when i strarted reading canadian i was turned on to bp nichol & bill bissett & the four horsemen crew who, like the beats & the dub poets, were fascinated with the human voice and with orality.

tho i don't write like any of the poets i've just mentioned, that's the route my early poetic interest took. music and oral poetry were present in equal measure with the literary.

## What is your working definition of a poem?

well, i haven't been writing much poetry lately. i've been into prose ... so perhaps my definition isn't working. it's being overhauled right now, re-designed, souped up. but for me the poetic engine is largely fired by language & sound. i used to call my writing "word sound systems," and i guess that term still applies. it's a literal definition: words are arranged into a sonic system. the system is guided by rhythm, melody, or a vowel or consonant pattern. words are often broken & misspelled & anagrammed & subjected to a series of rigorous manipulations. the system tests their performance – their ability to race in many different directions at once – to suggest multiple meanings & sounds. i guess you could say that for me, poetry is language in extreme high performance.

## Describe your writing ritual.

i used to hide myself away in my office, secret myself away from all distractions. then after a short while i'd pop out of the office to make a phone call. then i'd pop out to make some tea. then i'd pop out to take out the recycling. i wound up fighting to keep myself in the office & distraction out. now i just avoid my office. i place my laptop on the kitchen table, place the telephone next to the computer, turn on james brown, or memphis slim, take out some ingredients that i might want to cook with, and then sit down to write. since all of my distractions are within reach, i write. the music eventually gets turned off, the phone gets ignored, the ingredients get neglected, and i write.

## What is your approach to writing a poem?

i take a concrete, work-oriented approach to writing – the poems are gradually generated thru the sustained practice of writing. i apply myself to whatever ideas i have, be they formal or social or otherwise, and i work them out. i don't think about inspiration. what if it never arrives? what if it's late? what if i'm unable to recognize it when it strikes, or what if i'm unable to act on it because i'm at work, or asleep, or too bored, or out watching a prizefight? i'll take it if it comes, tho.

## Does being part of the English-speaking minority in Quebec impact on your writing?

i didn't grow up in québec, and as a writer i am not restricted to québec, so the language politics have had little impact on me. they did not shape my consciousness or my sense of being & belonging. i am also quite active outside of québec, and within québec much of my life is conducted in french. being a language-based minority in québec has little impact on my writing. it has much more impact on decisions like who i will publish with, or which funding bodies i feel i can have more success in applying to, or making sure to cultivate relationships with artists & organizations outside the province.

i am a minority in other ways: as a mixed-race canadian. one of my parents is irish canadian & the other is guyanese canadian, and that experience of being a minority has had much more impact on my writing.

much of my sound-poetry performance is not in any discernible language. it does not use words, but rather concentrates on phonemes and explores experiences of language that can be classified as highly stylized and carefully patterned gibberish. i am interested in the interstitial spaces between languages, the overlapping cadences, the places where speech errs and blurs between tongues.

## Do you think that writing in English in Quebec is a political act?

for an english writer, provincial boundaries dissolve. the nice thing abt writing & performing is that it can travel. if english writers were restricted to publishing & presenting their works in québec alone, then i might feel that working in english is a political act. but english writers can publish throughout north america; the markets for our work are much larger than the markets for french work. when my first book was published, it was launched in vancouver, ottawa, toronto, and montréal. further, i was eventually invited to read across the country – in halifax, calgary, gabriola (bc), saskatooooon, etc. i was interviewed on city tv in vancouver, on community radio in vancouver, on community radio in ottawa, and on cbc toronto. a french-language poet might get to launch a first volume in montréal, ottawa, and québec city, if lucky.

## Do you have a favourite Quebec poet?

nicole brossard. i like the way she challenges coherence & manipulates language, and i admire her ability to remain innovative for so many years. i've also seen her perform with jazz musicians. she met the volume of the instruments with her own vocal exertion, and she was physically invested in the performance, moving as she articulated. she fully sounded and embodied her writing, which is something that many poets avoid when they read.

## Do you write about Quebec?

i often write abt montréal. but about québec at large, no. maybe in coming works, maybe not.

## Why do you write?

I have said that writing is an exercise in freedom. that's definitely a romantic answer. writing is an exercise in creating and solving problems. the instant i begin to write, structural problems arise, problems related to coherence, problems related to cadence, etc, and attempting to solve them engages my faculties. i write to feel that deep engagement. if writing didn't engage me, i wouldn't do it.

## Who is your audience?

i've read my writing to people of all ages, from varied cultural backgrounds, from the west coast to the maritimes. the audience largely depends on the kind of event. the following is a generalizn – not always true, but often – if the event is more of a high-frequency performance poetry event where each poem goes 120 mph & breaks the sound barrier, the audience will be younger, 20somethns. if the event features authors who read from books instead of from memory, the audience will likely encompass boomers, gen x & even gen y. i've been invited to a wide range of events – folk festivals, lit fests, academic shindigs, poetry slams, cbc canada reads series, live remote broadcasts from suburban chapters, black community events & so forth – so i can't really say other than that my audience is likely a heterogeneous group. a mélange. a true north american gumbo, a creolized whole.

## Do you think there is an audience, outside of friends or other poets, for poetry?

yes definitely. if you consider poetry in all its guises, from rap thru lyric poetry thru avant-garde sound poetry thru folk music, you realize that nearly everyone comes into contact w poetry & nearly everyone is at some point an active audience member for poetry. the more you narrow your definition, the smaller your audience becomes.

## How does your day job impact on your writing?

it allows me to write without worrying abt how the bills will be paid.

## What is the toughest part of writing for you?

toughest part of writing is sitting down. i'm an active, athletic person who already spends countless work hours seated in front of a pc.

## Do you have a favourite time and place to write?

dining room table, early morning or late night. early morning with a cup of black tea & late night with a guinness.

KAIE KELLOUGH

## How many drafts do you usually go through before you are satisfied with a poem?

i don't know how many draughts i drown, but i am an obsessive ed.

## Do you write with the intention of "growing a manuscript" or do you work on individual poems that are later collected into a book?

i always start out with the idea of growing a manuscript, but while that inspires me it also defeats me & i wind up wound up & writing individual poems that are later carefully selected, collated, collected.

## What is your idea of a muse?

an interesting idea or clear observation. a disturbing incident or an incidental disturbance. anything that rivets or screws the mind.

## Do you like to travel? Is travel important to your writing?

in principle i love to travel, but in practice travel is a pain in the ass cuz it's expensive & uncomfortable & complicated. in the case of travel i am careful to let the principle guide the practice. travel is important to my writing bcuz it displaces & challenges identity. it disrupts routine, it places you in strange situations and demands that you reckon with those situations immediately. i find the same challenge in writing. i am not pleased when the vocabulary and the form become too familiar. i am constantly searching to out-reach my limits. both writing and travel encourage this. ∎

KAIE KELLOUGH

**échos**
*montréal nord, 11 août 2008*

**BLAMM** goes the service resolver. the unarmed brown boy oops

**BLAMM** echoes the **shock** through the **taut**-nerved borough

**BLAMM** echoes the crystal tear exploding from the duct

**BLAME** echoes the memory of anthony griffin, of marcellus wallace

**BLAMM** echoes the dark. night concusses the blue world

**BLAMM** echoes the eye-socket ruptured by a rock

**I AMM** echoes the molotov. glass flames scat

**BLAMM** echoes the *vitrine* fouled by *louisville* bat

**BLAMM** echo the bricks that batter the *urgence ambulance*

**BLAMM** echoes the slug of rum in the police captain's gut

**BLAMM** echoes the reporter's camera's cold mechanic shutter

**BLAMM** echoes the deadline

**BALMM** begs the dawn, **BALM.**

KAIE KELLOUGH

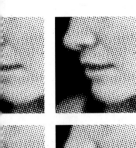

# Moe Clark

Photo: Kenneth Locke

Métis spoken word artist Moe Clark fuses her unique understanding of performance narrative with traditions of circle singing and spoken word. Her debut album is *Circle of She: Story & Song*. She appeared at the *IDEA World Congress: Art for Social Change* (Belem, Brazil, 2010), the *Maelström ReÉvolution Fiéstival* (Brussels, 2009), *Aboriginal Music Week* (Winnipeg, 2012), the *Makusham APTN Series* (Moncton, 2011), and the *Canadian Festival of Spoken Word* (2007, 2008, 2010). A featured speaker at *TedXMontreal* (2012), she performed for the Canadian Olympic Team at the *Olympic Summer Games* in London (2012). Her forthcoming album of words and music will appear in 2013. "Intersecting Circles," which appeared as a videopoem in 2009, is now part of the permanent collection at the *Peace River Museum, Archives and Mackenzie Centre.*

Clark also works as a community educator to facilitate voice, and conducts writing and spoken word workshops in high schools and local communities to promote literacy and creative expression.

### Poetry Quebec: Where are you originally from and why did you come to Quebec?

*Moe Clark:* Calgary, Alberta. I originally came to Quebec in June 2008 to find new stages for performance and poetry. I also came to collaborate with contemporary dancer, Jenn Doan, on the creation of a full-length voice and dance performance. Not even a month after moving here I was opening up for a show at the Fringe Festival and performing at Words & Music [Ian Ferrier's monthly show at Casa del Popolo]. This place just grew on me and offered me what Calgary couldn't – more artistic and cultural diversity!

### When did you encounter your first Quebec poem?

If by Quebec you mean Quebec writer/author that would have to be Leonard Cohen when I was first learning about Canadian poetry. In terms of my more recent years, I attended the Banff Centre's Spoken Word Program and got to meet Ian Ferrier, Catherine Kidd and D.Kimm.

### How did you first become interested in poetry?

Before I had a voice to speak the things I needed to share, I wrote them down. I remember keeping a journal when I was in elementary school. I used to be very shy. It wasn't until college that I really took an interest in spoken word and I did so through the Beats.

### Which of the Beats would you say most influenced you and what impact did they have on the way you began to write for performance?

I used to listen to Jack Kerouac's *On the Road* obsessively after I discovered a CD recording of it at my local Calgary public library. This was in first year of art school. Then after meeting Sheri-D Wilson in one of my classes, I learned so much more about the Beats through her work and stories. Years later, in Montreal, I got to meet and sing improvised vocals for Anne Waldman. When she performed her "Manitee" (Humanity) piece I was blown away and finally understood, in full depth, the relationship of the Beats to our collective spirit and to Buddhism.

### How does your Métis background influence your work?

Throughout my work I am constantly questioning identity and the role it plays in the creation of our "living mythologies." After discovering my Métis identity I began connecting to the communities in Alberta as well as drawing parallels to the way I was approaching song and my performance work. I've also always been a very spiritual person, and the rituals and ceremonies that I've taken part in from the Cree tradition (with Cree-Saulteaux origins) have greatly influenced how I approach performance. It becomes a ritual for me, as does the poetry that I write.

### What is your working definition of a poem?

Oh boy, it's constantly shifting and the more defined it gets, the more difficult it is to live up to that expectation. I'm always being challenged when I meet new poets and hear new forms of poetry. To me, a poem is something that brings an idea to life in an engaging, mythological, symbolic or metaphoric way. A poem is voicing how we live, why we live and what we live for. For me, poetry is breath.

### Do you call what you do poetry?

Yes. But it's not only poetry. It's hard to pull what we do from the boxes that society or arts funders want us to place it in.

### How does technology come into play in your work? How did you come to include it? What does it add?

I use technology in the performance and the documentation of my work. I'm constantly recording audio ideas on my iPhone or Zoom recording devices. Every time I go to test out a written poem (that's usually been edited on my Mac computer), I pull out the recording device as things grow and change when they are brought into a physical level of embodiment (sound). When I perform, I use a looping pedal to create environments of sound for the poetry to live within. I layer vocal experiments, put them through filter delays, construct, deconstruct the layers, until I have the right mix. From there I vocalize the poetry on top of it. For me, technology greatly supports my process by making it more adaptable to different environments and it helps me monitor what I'm doing and how I'm growing. When

MOE CLARK

I work with youth, it's a great asset to be able to create live beatboxing loops and bring that into freestyles and poetry.

## Since most of your work is oral/performance, do you feel the need for your work to be in print?

It's always important not to pigeonhole ourselves as artists. We do it enough writing grants. I love the written word and I see it being incredibly impactful as it carries another legacy of literature forward. Right now, I am working with a Marseillais poet on the translation of fifteen poems that will be in my first published book of poetry, in both English and French. This is incredibly important to me to broaden my scope and reach as an artist who is also bilingual, and to collaborate on fundamental ideas within my work through this process of translation of the written work. I think it's all about translation. Spoken word is just a translation of my ideas and written work into an embodied form. Song is a translation through the voice of our soul's work.

## Do you have a writing ritual?

I write when the idea comes. Sometimes I have blocks and I try to allow the block to be there and know they're not permanent (famous last words as a writer). One of my favourite "techniques" is the walking and recognizing technique. I take a walk outside as if everything I see is new and full of life that I am only now recognizing. I also really enjoy writing to music or writing from dreams. Dreams offer some of the richest and most fertile of images to draw our stories with.

## What is your approach to writing poems?

I am inspired by experiences, people I meet, things I'm constantly learning and relearning, living mythologies, dialogues with elders and members from my community, collaborations, and travelling. I tend to create poetry that is very visual in nature, inspired by my background in visual arts. I write a lot about and from my experiences during ritual and ceremonies. Or I write from my experiences as a woman, living in an urban space, inspired by strong women I meet and share and grow with. You could say it's social, thematic and inspiration-driven. When I pair the vocal aspect of the looping pedal with the written and then performed poetry, it becomes more about breaking and reassembling the structure of the written piece.

## Does being part of the English-speaking minority in Quebec influence how you write?

Not really. Canada is so much bigger than Quebec and I have found my voice even within that minority. I am grateful to be exposed to so many diverse languages in this province and city. Recently I have been trying to learn some Farsi so I can reinterpret Forough Farrokhzad's poetry. This initiative was inspired by my connection with Iranian-Canadian artist, Shahrzad Arshadi. We cross-pollinate as artists, which helps me find a bridge with not only the Persian language, but the culture as well. The only area that I find difficult is accessing funds as an anglophone artist. I haven't had a successful CALQ [Conseil des arts des lettres du Québec] application yet.

## Why haven't you been successful? Is this because of the experimental nature of your work or do you think that proportionately

**English-language writers aren't getting their fair share of the pie?**

I think to answer that would require a stronger knowledge, on my part, of the language polarities in Quebec. I will say though, that the Quebec government doesn't consider Métis people a sovereign nation. I largely think this has to do with the lack of education and knowledge in the Quebec government about Aboriginal sovereignty to clearly define our distinct histories as Aboriginal peoples.

**Do you think that writing in English in Quebec is a political act?**

Not for me. Unless someone is writing from a political lens or potentially if that person grew up here and was really involved in the transformation of Quebec as we know it. I moved here so recently that a lot of the conflict and rupture that's been happening has softened and there is more tolerance and inclusion of English artists now.

I have the great opportunity to direct the 2013 Canadian Festival of Spoken Word here in Montreal. This is an annual festival that travels across Canada each year, and brings to the stage over 120 slam poets, as well as feature spoken word artists and workshops, panels, etc., throughout the five-day festival. This year will be the first year the festival will be bilingual. We're working with the Literary Translators Association of Canada to ensure that every poet who attends will have the opportunity to have one poem translated in the other official language. It's a great amount of work, but an exciting opportunity for Canadian poetry as it is momentum towards a more inclusive "poetic society."

**Why do you write?**

To write the unspoken, to stay alive, to keep my mind active and moving, to learn and grow, to inspire.

**What piqued your interest in interdisciplinary performance poetry?**

Having a background in multiple performance vocabularies inspired me to find out how far I could take these languages into my poetic performance. First time I saw D.Kimm and Alexis O'Hara perform, I was really inspired by their use of technology. I am also really intrigued with projection work and shadow work. How can we create poetry with images and movement? And, of sound: How can we express ourselves without words and only using voice and sounds that are created [or] improvised in the moment? These are questions that drive my work. Ultimately, I don't like to restrict myself in any one medium. I want to connect and communicate, so I'll try almost any artistic means necessary to do so.

**Who is your audience?**

Everyone willing to listen: It varies on the day, the show or the moment. I've done shows for at-risk teenagers, for spiritual

143

MOE CLARK

gatherings, for my conservative parents, for Olympic athletes. Most recently, my most interesting performance moment was performing in a cafeteria for a group of elementary school kids in Gatineau, my poem about the residential schools. Normally, this wouldn't be the environment for such a heavy topic, but these youth were informed about the historical truths and they were able to connect and understand the poem. They actually asked for more.

## Do you think there is an audience, outside of friends or other poets, for poetry/spoken word?

Yes. Of course. Always. This is often the most rewarding space to perform in, when people have "never heard anything like it." Great! Not like I'm reinventing the wheel, but at least opening minds a bit further.

## What responsibility, if any, do poets have towards society?

It really depends on the poet and how far they want to reach out beyond themselves. Poetry can exist for only the creator, or it can go beyond that. The very act of writing and expressing a voice that otherwise wouldn't find itself, is a service to society, since it frees up space in our collective unconscious. For me, I take great care that the voice I am speaking from and with is as authentic and aware as possible. We have the power to change people's minds, to affect them in greater ways than a political speech or a commercial could, by activating the soul's voice. Someone once asked me why I've stayed a poet for so long, when "really, isn't poetry the poorest of the art forms?" I instantly laughed, [and] disagreed, since I think it's one of the richest ways to connect to our truth.

## How many drafts do you usually go through before you are satisfied with a piece?

Varies completely depending on the piece. My process usually requires a few written drafts, taking it to performance, then editing of drafts again.

## What is the toughest part of writing for you?

When I have a great idea and images in my mind, but the words seem to fall away. It's like a good dream that you remember when you first wake up, but forget later on, only remembering there was once something there that was lucid and vivid. This is why I should always write it down in the moment it comes.

## What is your idea of a muse?

Something, someone that tantalizes the mind, the ideas. Someone or something I can go to for inspiration. Sometimes it's a tangible thing or person, and sometimes just a big old tree or a great piece of music.

## Is travel important to your writing?

I love to travel one day, and hate it the next. Being in a space of transition often inspires writing that would otherwise not come through. Body and spirit in an unfixed place creates movement within that inspires new languages for embodying experience. I love language, culture, and finding myself in strange or unknown situations. These can bring about a great tension. When I'm constantly on the road though, I miss the comfort of my space, my bed, and my friends.

## Do you have a favourite Quebec poet?

I fell in love with José Acquelin's work the first moment I heard and met him at the Banff Centre. I don't get the opportunity to go to many of his shows, but each

MOE CLARK

time I've heard him perform and read his work, it's inspired my inner shamanic voice. There is a sense of ease and of presence in his work. It's light but has great depth.

**For the past few years, you've been involved in a program called "Writers in the Community" run by the Quebec Writers' Federation in collaboration with the Centre for Literacy of Quebec [WIC brings the literary arts to young people who are left out of the artistic mainstream]. How do you see your role in it? Describe some of the challenges and rewards of doing this kind of work.**

I've been participating in the project since last spring 2011. It's a great initiative that I am honoured to be part of. For me, almost all of the moments are memorable. I have the chance to work with youth who come from all different walks of life, and they are constantly teaching me things I never would have otherwise learned. One student brought in his poem about his life growing up in Park Ex. Attached to the piece was a news article about Freddy Villanueva, a young man who was shot by police in the local park. Another student, who I had the chance to teach via video conferencing in a remote community of Val D'Or Quebec, wrote about her experiences being a residential school survivor. At our "chapbook launch" we were all gathered around talking, and she said that after finding out she had a great-aunt who was a writer, she knew that now it's her turn to carry on that legacy.

**Based on your work with "Writers in the Community" do you think that poetry can affect someone's life?**

As a poet, I think it's pretty evident the importance of poetry and performance throughout the ages. In our contemporary society it is really important as educators/poets to find ways to cross-pollinate our methodologies of understanding what poetry is and can be. Looking at the collective experience, the hip-hop or "urban" experience can bring a lot of space for expression. If there is even a small chance for someone to feel more empowered in their own experience, then yes, poetry changes lives. ∎

### Twist Tobacco

***I know what it means to burn tobacco***
***but do I know what it means to twist it?***

Rewind bloodlines
of soil, sun and prayer
wrap spirit up in form
to create an arm of refuge
for this story to grow

*We gather*
> In Autumn's amber breeze
> a waxing moon
> through the windows of trees

*We occupy mountains*
> flat as pavement painted with lines
> together we mend
> a wet wrap of solidarity

*We gather*
> braid our spirits with sacred spit
> for our missing sisters and stolen lands
> celebrate the strength of their wombs
> that suffer colonial demands

Their bodies erode from tainted roots:
"savage, dirty, squaw"
product placements,
they are products of being placed
on reserves and residential schools
Our nations loose oil reserves
then make more Indian ones,
dam their land with hydroelectric walls
stutter the landscape with persistence

But we gather
*trade borders of fear*
*for altars of hope*

MOE CLARK

It is here she steps into our embrace
exchanges abandon for belonging

> *She* is fossilized story
> thrown to water
> skipping then sinking deep

> *She* is spirit screaming
> between words of prayer
> her cry blooms for open ears

> *She* is ghost
> scent of whiskey, sour milk, tundra
> shame her skin as she goes in

What deeds have stolen the land of her body
time and time again, the systemic occupation
of her hands and feet, tongue and teeth
making alien marrow from bone

**I know what it means to burn tobacco**
**but do we know what it means to twist it?**

I find breath
Shed a mountain of myself
Face forward, honour this land
*Do you hear me?*
No drum – no megaphone
only hearts alone
beating

**Listen**    *Do you hear me?*

> I step up to the song of her cry
> ancient child wailing
> fierce phoenix quaking
> in hearts soft mould

**Listen**   Do you hear me?

   I step up to the song of her cry
   whisper of white wind
   revolution of red wings
   our collective ancestry

**Listen**   Do you hear me?

   I sing out Strong Woman's Song
   a cry created from behind prison walls
   to honour the strength
   of Aboriginal Women

Like moon she rotates
her silver cry begins to sing      *along*
face to face                       *in song*
She sees her light full            *of dignity*
We align to strengthen             *community*

Intertwine *invisible* legacies
like tobacco twisting
*spirit*

**Listen**
*Do you hear it?*

I – tactile voice, give rise to possibility
to the promise of choice.

**Because I know what it means to burn tobacco**
**but do you know what it means to twist it?**

MOE CLARK

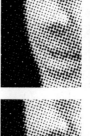

# Jason Camlot

Jason Camlot is the author of three collections of poetry, *The Debaucher* (Insomniac Press, 2008), *Attention All Typewriters* (DC Books, 2005), and *The Animal Library* (DC Books, 2001). A new book of poems entitled *What the World Said* will appear with Mansfield Press in 2013. His critical works include *Style and the Nineteenth-Century British Critic* (Ashgate, 2008) and *Language Acts: Anglo-Québec Poetry, 1976 to the Twenty-First Century* (Véhicule Press, 2007), co-edited with Todd Swift. He teaches Victorian literature at Concordia University in Montreal.

JASON CAMLOT

**Poetry Quebec: Where are you from?**

*Jason Camlot:* I was born in Montreal. My parents were born in Quebec, as well.

**When did you encounter your first Quebec poem?**

The first "Quebec" poem I encountered was recited to me when I was a kid by my father who was not really a poetry ↗

reader. It was "De Habitant" by William Henry Drummond, a dialect poem that was written to capture the French habitant's manner of speaking English. It's not a poem that has fared well, reputation-wise, for obvious reasons, but it is a pretty typical specimen of popular, 19th century dialect poetry, and my father really appreciated what Drummond was doing:

De place I get born, me, is up on de reever
Near foot of de rapide dat's call Cheval Blanc
Beeg mountain behin' it, so high you can't climb it
An' whole place she's mebbe two honder arpent.

↙

My father was raised, early on, in Senneterre, which is a town in the Abitibi region of northwestern Quebec. His father and his uncle had a trading post (general store) there at the time. My father also had cousins who lived in

Lac St. Jean. His extended family was involved in the fur trade – which became my father's business, as well. So, he had personal history in the northern regions of Quebec. He had a great love of the French province and language. When he came of age to go to school (around the age of six), his parents wanted him to be bilingual, so they moved into Montreal. His spoken French was equal to his English, and even when he was in his late teens, courting my mother in what we now call the Plateau and Mile End districts of Montreal, he would still often mix French and English in his speech. I think these facts of his early upbringing are why he enjoyed Drummond's poetry so much.

The next "Quebec" poem I encountered was the result of the fact that ↗

the guidance counselor of my high school was A.M. Klein's daughter-in-law. I was writing poetry of my own by this time and was intrigued to know the relative of a *real*, published poet. So, I borrowed A.M. Klein's *The Rocking Chair and Other Poems* from my high school library and tried to make sense of what I found in that amazing book. In some ways it was a modernist, or more specifically, Joycean, continuation of the bilingual language play I had first encountered in Drummond's poetry:

> O city metropole, isle riverain!
> Your ancient pavages and sainted routs
> Treverse my spirit's conjured avenues!
> Splendour erablic of your promenades
> Foliates there, and there your maisonry
> Of pendant balcon and scalier'd march...

↙

JASON CAMLOT

### How did you first become interested in poetry?

I first became interested in song lyrics and then in poetry. I came from a fairly musical family. My mother played piano, my father loved to sing (and had a nice voice), one of my older sisters was a professional singer for a short while, and the other was a music major at university. We did a lot of guitar playing and harmonizing on popular songs at home, sentimental tunes like "Donna Donna" (originally a Yiddish theatre tune called "Dos Kelbl"), Mary Hopkin's "Those Were the Days, My Friend," as well as lots of Beatles, Bob Dylan and Cat Stevens songs. Being the youngest by seven years, with two older sisters who were teenagers in the early '70s, I inherited a lot of vinyl and listened to a lot of folk

and pop music when I was very young. In elementary school, I was obsessively collecting Beatles records when my friends were going to Discus to purchase Boney M.'s "Rasputin" or "Funky Town" by Lipps Inc. (Not that I wasn't into disco, too.) I started playing guitar at the age of eight and began writing songs as soon as I could play three chords (D, A, E). The first song I wrote was "Blind Superman," a narrative ballad based on the story of the 1972 film *Butterflies Are Free* (starring Edward Albert and Goldie Hawn!) about a young blind man who moves out to live on his own. I have continued to write songs to this day. The first poetry I wrote without music was a combination of the Beatles and Dylan lyrics I was listening to and the biblical language I was encountering through my parochial school education. Consequently, it was brooding, used concrete imagery, and attempted to be allegorical.

## What is your working definition of a poem?

A poem is when language does something amazing for no particular reason.

## Why do you write?

I write because once in a while I enjoy the process, and occasionally I enjoy the outcome. These sporadic moments of gratification are enough to keep the hamster wheel spinning.

## Do you have a writing ritual?

I write *something* every single day, even if it's just an epigram or an entry in my nerve diary (these entries consisting of three lines of three words each). I've been tweeting poems based on words randomly chosen from the *Merriam-Webster Dictionary* lately. Just entering that frame of mind for a period, even if only for several moments, is important to my health and well-being.

## What is your approach to writing a poem?

My approach to writing really depends upon the project I'm engaged in. I am often inspired by the discursive registers of rather esoteric works of non-fiction, and, increasingly, by the vast and variegated linguistic flower gardens delivered by search engines.

## What is the toughest part of writing for you?

The sitting part. I find sitting uncomfortable. I sometimes stand when I write, but I find it easier to write while sitting down, which is due to habits formed at a young age, I'm sure.

## Do you think that being part of the English-speaking a minority in Quebec affects your writing?

As I am immersed in the political and linguistic situation of Quebec, I am sure it affects my writing in particular ways, just as being immersed in the political situations of Boston and San Francisco affected my writing in particular ways when I lived in those places. The "how" question is too complicated for this forum, as it would entail adding Methylene Blue dye to the historical cells and forces around me and then trying to make sense of what shows up.

## Do you think that writing in English in Quebec is a political act?

There are occasions I can imagine for which writing in English in Quebec would be perceived as a political act – for example, if I were a shop owner and made a point of writing my signage in English only. This would be against the laws of the province and thus could be identified as an overtly political use of the English language within the Quebec context. But that example doesn't really apply to me. As far as the use of English in the writing of poetry goes, I do believe that when Michèle Lalonde used English in her poem "Speak White" and read it before an audience of thousands at the first Nuit de la poésie in Montreal in 1970, she was engaged in a politically-motivated language act, and that the use of English in her poem was received as a political act by her audience. In other words, I think that the context of production and reception have a lot to do with whether writing in English in Quebec functions as a political act.

## Do you write about Quebec?

I don't consciously write about Quebec, the way Gilles Vigneault or Pierre Nepveu has written (each in his own way) about Quebec, or the way, say, Al Purdy wrote about certain places in Canada. But I have used the word *dépanneur* at least once in a poem of my own composition.

## Who is your audience?

"Audience" seems too grandiose a term for the people who read and listen to my poetry. I really have little sense of who reads what I write, other than the people I see at the readings I give – mostly students, fellow poets and artists, and occasionally, colleagues and family members.

## Do you think there is an audience, outside of friends or other poets, for poetry?

There's family. I would definitely add family members to the list you have provided. And aspiring poets.

## What is your idea of a muse?

Found language, for one thing.

## Do you have a favourite time and place to write?

When I am travelling and away from home I like to write in a public library or a quiet café. At home, I like to write at the kitchen table, especially late at night when I am awake and everyone else is sleeping. At work, I like to write at my desk with the light off so that no one knows I'm actually in the office.

## Is travel is important to your writing?

Yes, I love to travel and to write in strange places using the foreign notebooks and stationary that one can purchase while abroad. Sometimes the right notepad or pen purchased in a foreign place can inspire an entire series of new forms or voices, as when I spent a month in Oxford (UK), purchased a pad of textured British Imperial-sized onion paper,

and filled the pad up with Oxbridgey-sounding nonsense poems.

## Does your day job at Concordia University impact on your writing?

I am a literature professor. I read poetry every day as part of my job. I talk about poetry and write about poetry pretty much every day, as part of my job. I am surrounded by adult colleagues who read, talk and write about poetry every day as part of their jobs, and by students who are studying poetry, learning to talk and write about it, and, sometimes, to write it, as well. Further, because my department encourages the coordination of poetry readings and talks about literature and poetry, I am frequently involved, either as an organizer or participant, in such events. For all of these reasons I'd say that my day job encourages my continued participation and interest in poetry-related activities. It feeds my habit.

## Why did you decide to take on the job of poetry editor for DC Books?

My former colleague and friend, the poet and novelist Robert Allen had been poetry and fiction editor of the DC Books "New Writers Series" imprint for many years. Following Rob's death in 2006, DC Books publisher Steve Luxton approached me to take over the imprint in both genres. I was very interested in taking over the poetry imprint, but didn't feel I had the time (or the expertise, as Rob had had) to edit in both genres. DC Books meant a lot to me. My first book of poems came out with DC in the imprint Rob edited. Beyond that, I knew that DC Books had an interesting place in the history of Montreal small press publishing. Founded by Louis Dudek in the 1970s, it represented a continuation of publishing

JASON CAMLOT

projects like Contact and Delta Canada that Dudek had been involved in during the two previous decades, all of which were attempts to provide support for innovative Canadian writing. Some of the earliest DC titles included Avi Boxer's *No Address* (1971), John Glassco's *Montreal* (1973), an oddly biting collection of poems by Harry Howith with the perfectly hilarious title, *The Stately Homes of Westmount* (1973), as well as several titles by Dudek, himself. In its early years, DC under Dudek, seemed especially interested in positioning local writers in relation to the new modes of writing that were emerging across North America. Rob Allen's imprint also focused on young talent from Montreal, including first publications by writers such as Anne Stone, Barrie Sherwood, Dimitri Nasrallah and Heather O'Neill, and, again, experimental titles of his own fiction and poetry such as the poetry collection *Ricky Ricardo Suites* (2000), and his masterpiece of poetic prose, *Napolean's Retreat* (1997). Rob's taste for the imprint he edited in both fiction and poetry was extremely diverse, but always seemed to champion young writers who were working somewhere outside or against the grain of recent trends in Canadian writing. This seemed to fit well with the spirit of the press as Dudek had originally imagined it, and this was something I could get behind, as well. I asked my good friend, poet and fiction writer David McGimpsey if he would be willing to edit the fiction side of a new imprint for DC Books. Dave agreed, and so I pitched the idea for the Punchy Writers Series (Jason Camlot, poetry editor, David McGimpsey, fiction editor) to Steve Luxton and Keith Henderson.

They liked the idea and we were off to the races.

**Does being an English-language poetry press in Montreal pose special challenges in getting manuscripts and attention from outside of Quebec?**

I think it may limit the number of queries we get simply because some writers wouldn't think of publishing with a small Montreal-based press like DC. I have to go out and solicit things a bit more, and then try to convince authors (especially more established ones) that there will be benefits to publishing a Punchy Writers Series book. And sometimes writers are really intrigued by that prospect. Stuart·Ross was genuinely interested in publishing something out of Montreal since he hadn't done that before. Our location also allows us to benefit significantly from the wealth of talented young writers who come through the Concordia Creative Writing program, many of whom stick around afterwards. So in that sense, we have access to some great local talent as a result of our being an English-language poetry press in Montreal. As far as exposure goes, DC is a very small press and we do our best to get the word out for our books at a grassroots level, using Facebook, poetry readings, that sort of thing. Many of our authors are fantastic at creating opportunities for themselves and are just deeply invested in finding ways to share their work through touring and reading, so that has helped a lot. There's a vibrant series of readings that occur in Montreal, and our authors benefit from that. We've also had great support from friends like rob mclennan in Ottawa, and series like The Pivot, in Toronto, over the years. I'd love to get our writers out to Vancouver, Winnipeg, Halifax, more, but this is a wish I imagine is shared by many other small presses.

## What do you look for in a manuscript?

I, personally, look for something daring and strange that resonates with me as both true and truly bizarre. Check out the first couple of titles I edited for the imprint, Stuart Ross's *Dead Cars in Managua* and Angela Szczepaniak's *Unisex Love Poems*, and you'll get a sense of what I'm talking about. Stuart's book is really three mini-books in one: a surreal guidebook to Managua with accompanying photos of destroyed automobiles, a long suite of poems that capture the untenable temporality of hospitals, and a collection of experimental poems that were written using the composition techniques he explores in his poetry boot camps. Angela's book is a 180-page novel in verse that features a collage of etiquette advice, illustrated love organ recipes, typeface cartoons, field notes concerned with the cause of an h-rash (a rash that manifests itself as clusters of the letter h on the body), and a melodrama about a couple of inch-tall lawyers, to name just a few of its incredible elements. So, we're looking for stuff like that.

## What do you expect from the writers that you are working with?

I want the writers I work with to understand that they are artists, and to approach the project we're working on with seriousness and with the sense of "fuck-you" daring that should come with being an artist.

## What are your own aesthetics when it comes to poetry?

Eclectic and in-between. I am interested in a great variety of poetic modes and affective registers. I am interested in formal (and medial) experimentation and I am interested in poetic forms that have accrued some authority over the centuries, and trying new things with them. I am interested in non-sense and I am deeply invested in the powers and payoffs of "meaning." I like when these two functions of language work in tandem to create powerful, felt effects. I like weird, beautiful voices, and often these voices emerge when language is allowed to speak according to its own artificial logic. I am interested in poetry as a medium of pleasure, an opportunity for play, and as a bold, blunt instrument that clears the way for havoc and adventure.

## How does being a poet in your own right affect your manuscript choices?

Certainly I choose manuscripts that I love, personally. I think I'm attracted to projects that I wish I could have written myself. I remember presenting Stuart Ross's work at a reading he couldn't attend himself. I read a poem from *Dead Cars in Managua* and when the reading was done I said out loud (without realizing I was speaking what I was thinking), "Fuck, I wish I'd written that one." It's especially fun when editing becomes a way for me to participate in the creation of a book that I could never have written myself. ∎

JASON CAMLOT

## Bewildered Alexandrines

Dazed speechless baffled flabbergasted mazed misled
Dumbfounded struck rebounded rattled in the head

Blind muddled hit befuddled knocked floored blown-breathless
Strewn puzzled flipped bedazzled into nothingness

Agape bamboozled battered wrecked confuséd lost
Addled shook confounded fazed hazy horror-tossed

Dismayed forlorn spun whirling ruffled to the core
Thrown flustered off bothered perplexed looking for more

Shamed crushed embarrassed burnt cut reeling fucked
Staggering awed astounded woozy wonderstruck

Disgraced aghast disturbed astonished stupefied
Afraid left in the dark bewildered but alive

## The Spades

*Le gel durcit les eaux...*

*Street puddles harden;*
*souvlaki-joint windows whiten with frost.*

To the east on St. Catherine girls invade
the Burger King, or scuttle in rhinestone
heels like catwalk models in an air-raid
toward *dépanneurs*, or into taxis home.

Wads of filthy, frozen gum look like dead
toads on the street, plastic straws like striped reeds
rolling under cars. A slow kick drum beats
heavily for a moment, then recedes.

Now the clubs are closed. Vacuum *camionettes*
suck up waste through huge, corrugated snouts.
A shirtless Hoosick (NY) frosh scrambles a deck
of playing cards reduced to just one suit.

No clubs, diamonds, no hearts, just trembling spades
floating the street. An ominous parade.

*After Émile Verhaeren's "La Bêche"*

JASON CAMLOT

# Gillian Sze

**Gillian Sze is the author of *The Anatomy of Clay* (ECW Press, 2011) and *Fish Bones* (DC Books, 2009), which was shortlisted for the QWF McAuslan First Book Prize in 2009, as well as three chapbooks: *This is the Colour I Love You Best* (2007), *A Tender Invention* (2008), and *Allow Me to Conjugate* (2010). She co-founded *Branch Magazine*, an online magazine showcasing Canadian art, design and writing, and is currently working on a Ph.D. at Université de Montréal. Her next book, *Peeling Rambutan*, is forthcoming from Gaspereau Press in 2014.**

**Poetry Quebec: You aren't a Quebecer by birth. Why did you come here?**

*Gillian Sze:* I was born and raised in Winnipeg and came here, partly to get away from it, partly for love, partly for school. I did my B.A. and M.A. at Concordia, tried out Toronto for a bit, but found myself returning.

**When did you first become interested in poetry?**

It started early, when I was about six and Shel Silverstein was my Virgil. We also had to memorize poems from Maurice Sendak's *Chicken Soup with Rice*. I thought that was the best book ever at the time. *Where the Sidewalk Ends* is still up there for me.

**What was your first encounter with a Quebec poem?**

I believe it was Leonard Cohen's "You Have the Lovers." I was maybe fifteen at the time. The poem was in a collection of 20th century poetry, which I still have. My father had bought it used for a dollar. Irving Layton and A. M. Klein are in there, too.

**Do you write about Quebec?**

My poem, "fragmented," in *Fish Bones* is a strange homage to Montreal. My most recent chapbook, *Allow Me to Conjugate*, is set in Quebec. Place is dependent on, if not just as important as, experience. When I moved here, for instance, I was feeling terribly homesick, and to express that, all I could write about was Winnipeg. (Dis)locations always creep into my work.

**Would you say that writing in English in Quebec is a political act?**

It isn't the impetus for me. I write because I want to connect, and usually in the simplest way possible.

## What is your working definition of a poem?

I fall somewhere between William Carlos Williams and Elizabeth Bishop. Williams says that "a poem is made up of words and the spaces between them," and Bishop, that it's "hundreds of things coming together at the right moment." A poem, for me, is all of that: words, spaces, many things, and perfect timing.

## Do you have a writing ritual?

Not really. I like to flip through other poetry books. Visit galleries and museums. People-watch. Clear the clutter from my desk. Have a decent stretch of time ahead of me where some quiet and privacy are guaranteed.

## Why do you write?

Because I can't not.

> I am all middle-ground,
> flanked by the urgency of language,
> the tremor
> and the salacity that swings above it.
> — from "Lunacy," *Fish Bones*

## Who is your audience?

The idea of an audience is always abstract. The audience is an unnamed "someone" that I let my work deal with first.

## Do you think there is an audience, outside of friends or other poets, for poetry?

Of course. Poetry isn't marketed like popular television, but an audience is out there. Furthermore, with the invention of the "retweet," there has probably never been more rapid transmission and retransmission of shards of poetry.

**You collaborate with Roberutsu, a multidisciplinary designer from the Canadian Prairies on *Branch Magazine,* a national online publication devoted to exploring the rifts and overlaps of visual and literary arts. Why did you start it and how has working on this magazine fuelled your own poetry, if at all?**

In 2009, when I was living in Toronto and Rob was still in Winnipeg, we discussed starting up an online zine. After years of working individually and collaboratively, we both felt that it was time to turn to our creative friends, influences and obsessions and dedicate a small corner of the Internet to them. We took a year to form the basic plan of our project, create some buzz around *Branch*, and finally launch our first issue the following spring.

Right now we're both students – when we first started, Rob was working a full-time job as an art director – and *Branch* is obviously a labour of love since it's something we do on the side when we're not working on our own personal projects. We logged our hours once and calculated that each issue takes about sixty hours. It's a chunk of time, but it's rewarding. *Branch* is good for us because it keeps us thinking creatively and engaged with what's out there. And if there's one thing we learned, it's that there's *a lot* out there.

**What is your approach to the writing of poems: inspiration driven, structural, social, thematic... ?**

All of the above. I can be moved by a scene, another poem, the weather, nostalgia. Ultimately, I write so I don't have

GILLIAN SZE

to experience the nauseating retention of not writing.

**That echoes the quote by Maya Angelou posted on the website of *Branch Magazine*: "There is no agony like bearing an untold story inside you." For you, how does "the nauseating retention of not writing" manifest itself?**

I guess for me it's just a general sense of dissatisfaction and guilt that's reminiscent of taking weeks off the gym. It's a sort of private sheepishness that lingers.

**Does being part of the English-speaking minority in Quebec influence what or how you write?**

Not being from Quebec, I never grew up with the French-English tensions that other English writers writing in this province are familiar with. I grew up with my own language tensions, certainly, but a poet is a minority wherever she is.

**Does any aspect of your Asian heritage figure into your poetry?**

Absolutely. Everything about me – "about" in all senses – figures into my work. And that, of course, includes the cultures I've grown up in and encountered. It was only when I got older that I stepped back and appreciated the peculiarities and nuances of my Chinese culture that I had, until then, deemed ordinary. Like celebrating two new years, eating longevity noodles on your birthday, or, after breaking down the phrase, realizing that when your mother was telling you to be careful, she was always saying, "small heart." Part of our Saturday Chinese school curriculum was reciting Chinese poetry, so that was another rich literary source. Chinese

culture is something I've always rubbed up against. It's both very familiar and, at the same time, very alien to me. My latest project, *Peeling Rambutan*, is based on my first trip to China and deals with precisely this phenomenon. Where we come from is a common subject for anyone, and while it has always made its way into my work in the past, now it's something I'm aware of, something I consciously explore, linguistically and historically.

**You are currently pursuing a Ph.D. at Université de Montréal. Is your thesis poetry related?**

My focus right now is on classical reception and the use of Greek fragments in modernist and contemporary poetry. My areas of interest include the literary archives, classical history, modernism and the poetics of loss and error.

**Does being a full-time student interfere with or invigorate your writing process?**

It does both. Balancing school with writing was a major concern of mine when I first started the program but, increasingly, I'm able to have academic work feed into creative activity. Charles Simic says that poetry attracts him "because it makes trouble for thinkers." I agree; no matter how I handle a poem, I always come across some resistance, whether it's grappling with another poet's sense, or attempting to convey my own. I suppose this is what Simic calls "trouble."

**How many drafts do you usually go through before you are satisfied with a poem?**

It varies. I never get it right the first time. It's a miracle, or an accident, if I even get it close. I've spent as little as one week and as long as six years on a poem.

**Do you write with the intention of "growing a manuscript" or do you work on individual poems that are later collected into a book?**

When I write, the most pressing concern in that moment is the poem itself. I'm just working for the poem. I've written with the intention of "growing a manuscript" and I sometimes have the sense of a larger manuscript on the horizon but I work best without those pressures.

**What is the toughest part of writing for you?**

The toughest part is to allow myself to begin with rubbish, to not think too much and just have a beginning.

**What is your idea of a muse?**

My muses are all the people I've fallen in love with and all the people I haven't yet, real or imaginary.

**Do you have a favourite time and place to write?**

I'm flexible. Just put me in a quiet space with good light and a few good books at hand.

**How does travel, if at all, act as a catalyst to your writing?**

I like travelling but I'm also a huge homebody. Otto Dix says "there is so much that is strange in what surrounds us that there is no reason to use or seek out new subjects." I think what is important is experience of any kind, whether it comes in the form of travel, narcotics, dreams, unpleasant moments, love, everydayness. I think what Dix is emphasizing is the artist's task to be sensitive to one's own surroundings, to be aware of the extraordinary beyond the ordinary.

Yes: she is ordinary, like most people;
but how lucky they are to witness
her miss the last tendril,
the one that sticks to her neck,
curled like a crescent moon.

– from "Bun," *The Anatomy of Clay*

***Fish Bones* is written in the ekphrastic tradition, but with a twist. Elsewhere, you have called the book "a collection of conversations." Can you elaborate on that?**

When I was writing *Fish Bones*, I was reading Jeanette Winterson's *Art Objects*. The first essay describes the intensity and discomfort associated with concentrating, examining, looking at a painting. But this "looking" is actually reciprocal. The painting looks *back* and Winterson describes this relationship as "a constant exchange of emotion between us, between the three of us; the artist I need never meet, the painting in its own right, and me, the one who loves it and can no longer live independent of it." And so for me, *Fish Bones* is not only a book of ekphrastic poems, but is a more complicated engagement with artworks and the artists. I cannot respond and act on the art without the art somehow acting on me. There is also something to be said about how time affects this "trialogue." How I look at a painting differs from a later experience, and an even later experience. "To John Lyman and the Portrait of His Father," probably best exemplifies this relationship of looking. I like the practice of ekphrasis for this exact reason. There's always someone or something out there who wants to talk.

I meant to write something that said,
*Yes, I know what you mean.*

Your father sitting there, dark and broad,
like the old rock at the riverfront by my house.
The deliberate crossing of his legs,
his spectacles balanced on a hard bridge,
a left elbow digging into the cushioned arm.

He's been keeping a shadow in his shirt pocket.

**Fish Bones** **was shortlisted for the 2009 McAuslan First Book Prize, awarded by the Quebec Writers' Federation. How did this nomination change or redirect your writing career?**

I was very honoured that *Fish Bones* made it that far. I've always had a habit of keeping expectations low so, at the time, I was just delighted to have a full-length collection out. I learned that Fred Wah was on the jury that year and as an admirer and as a new writer, it was quite humbling to know that he took the time to read it. The nomination was an unexpected and rewarding experi-ence but, to be honest, even if it didn't happen, I would still have continued to write. Since *Fish Bones*, I've served on several prize juries and learned quickly that the process is not only difficult, but also subjective, collaborative and com-plicated. When it comes down to a final agreement amongst the judges, luck, negotiation and compromise play their parts. So in terms of nominations and prizes changing my writing career, I'd say that for me, the primary concern is to get the words down as best I can. Everything that follows is out of my hands. The work takes a life of its own – and that's kind of exciting, isn't it? ∎

## Lunacy

Behind the buildings,
the sky is like verdigris above the horizon.
The last year rusted through, I wake early.
Raise my green tea to the moon.
It looks down with a half-closed eye.

Lately, I've been more aware
of the moon's phases.
We are somewhere between a new moon
and the first quarter,
and I find myself at intersections
seeking a sliver of shaded relief
behind the blinds.

I am all middle-ground,
flanked by the urgency of language,
the tremor
and the salacity that swings above it.

A full moon will sprout in two weeks.
They say its effects usually last for four days.
People on the street will shift just as I pass,
this dementia will be a lighter bearing.

## Roses

*It was the kind of morning*
*the dark never left.*
        – Stephen Dunn

Clandestine roses have appeared
in her pasta jars and cooled kettles of forgotten water.
They've been stuck in dusty wine bottles,
crammed to the back of her fridge,
strewn across piano keys.
A bouquet in each slipper.
Petals in the toaster.

She blossoms onto the subway
and unfolds rosebuds from her pockets.
A boy tows potted roses behind him on his skateboard.
The scent cuts the underground desert,
the forlorn winter,
the fog.

163

GILLIAN SZE

# Angela Leuck

Photo: Angela Leuck

Award winning haiku and tanka poet Angela Leuck has been pub-
lished in journals and anthologies worldwide. Her poems were includ-
ed in *Haiku Journey*, a video game by Hot Lava Games (2006). The au-
thor of *Garden Meditations* and *a cicada in the cosmos* (inkling press,
2010), *haiku white* and *haiku noir* (carve, 2007) and *Flower Heart*
(Blue Ginkgo Press, 2006), she also edited numerous anthologies, in-
cluding *Rose Haiku for Flower Lovers and Gardeners* (Price-Patterson,
2005), *Tulip Haiku* (Shoreline, 2004), and, with Maxianne Berger, *Sun
Through the Blinds: Montreal Haiku Today* (Shoreline, 2003).

She has read and led numerous workshops at schools, libraries and
conferences, and participated in the national *Random Acts of Poetry*
project in 2007 and 2010. She is the founder and organizer of the Black
Tea Haiku Group in Montreal and is the Quebec Regional Coordinator
for Haiku Canada. In 2005, with Kozue Uzawa, she co-founded Tanka
Canada and its biannual journal *Gusts*.

***Poetry Quebec:* Where are you
originally from?**

Angela Leuck: I was born in Vancouver
in 1960 and grew up in Lillooet, a small
town in the Fraser Canyon. Lillooet is
famous for being Mile 0 of the first great
BC gold rush of 1858–59. Infamously,
during the Second World War, it was
also the site of a relocation camp for
Japanese-Canadians. After the war,
some of the internees remained and
their sons and daughters were my class-
mates. Through them, I gained my intro-
duction to Japanese culture.

**How did you end up in Quebec?**

When I was sixteen, my parents
retired to Saskatoon. Moving from the
mountains of BC to the prairie was a
shock, but after a few years I grew to
love the open spaces and simplicity of
the landscape. I attended the University
of Saskatchewan and completed a B.A.
in Economics in 1983, then accepted
a scholarship to do graduate work at
McGill. Coming to Montreal changed
everything. I was drawn to its vibrant
literary and artistic life. By the time I
graduated with my M.A., I was no longer

an economist – I was a writer and well on my way to becoming a poet!

## When did you encounter your first Quebec poem?

The first collection of poems by a Quebecer that caught my attention was *Diary of a Trademark* by Ian Stephens. I was living in St. Henri at the time, and his poems, such as the one about The New System Restaurant, showed me the power of poetry to transform the simple experience of eating in a working-class greasy spoon into something profound. It made me realize that what poets do is make us see our lives have deeper meaning, and even our seemingly most mundane moments can be significant.

## Who is your favourite Quebec poet?

My favourite Quebec poet is Steve Luxton. He's also my husband so I'm prejudiced in his favour, but he really is my favourite poet, because of his knowledge, experience and sincere dedication to poetry.

## When did you first become interested in poetry?

When I was in grade 5, my teacher introduced the class to haiku. He explained its few simple rules, then sent us out into nature to observe and write. It was fun and freeing. I can't remember anything else we studied in English that year, but haiku really stuck. I rediscovered it in my early thirties, when, as a single parent with an autistic child, I didn't have a lot of time or emotional energy to put into my writing. I found I could fit haiku into my busy life. As well, haiku's focus on the seasons and the natural world helped me develop a more Zen-like detachment from the stresses I needed to face. Later I encountered another Japanese poetry form called tanka, a five-line Japanese lyric poem with a 1400-year history. Tanka is concerned with feeling, and writing it allowed me to be both creative and have a rich emotional life.

## What is your working definition of a poem?

The poetry I write has been mostly haiku and tanka. Both follow a clearly defined form in Japanese that has had to be adapted to the nuances of English. There is still much controversy among English-language haiku and tanka poets about how these forms can be carried over into English, but it's pretty clear a certain spirit defines each and you can say this is a haiku and another three-liner isn't – it's a free-form poem. For me, a haiku is a poem generally not exceeding seventeen syllables and about a moment in time. It may or may not refer to the season or nature, but always employs one or two concrete images. A tanka, two lines longer and less than thirty-one syllables, is a much freer lyric form and is concerned with capturing a strongly felt emotion.

## What is your approach to writing poems?

Lately, I write thematically. My most significant theme has been gardens and flowers. But there are other themes, such as love and jazz, which resonate with me.

## Do you have a writing ritual?

I have various rituals that change over time. I maintain a ritual for as long as it works. For instance, I used to take a morning haiku walk around Rutherford Park above McGill University. I would circle the track, observing changes in the seasons or weather. These gave me inspiration for my haiku. For a year, I also visited the Japanese Garden of the Montreal Botanical Garden once a week and wrote about it throughout the seasons. Another time, I took walks along the St. Lawrence River in Verdun, where a friend and I would get together every Saturday and share our poems. Now I write because I lead Montreal's Black Tea Haiku Group and I bring poems to our monthly meetings. Our workshops are in the form of a Japanese "kukai" consisting of a number of highly developed rituals that connect us to the Japanese tradition.

## Do you think that being part of the English-speaking minority in Quebec influences your writing?

As a haiku and tanka poet, I am a minority within the mainstream poetry world, which in a way mimics being a minority writer in a broader sense. Haiku and tanka are still largely ghettoized within the poetry world. This has its advantages, having led to the growth of a flourishing haiku and tanka community with publications that are geared just for these forms. On the national level, we have Haiku Canada with a membership of nearly 200 poets, while in 2005, Kozue Uzawa and I founded Tanka Canada and its biannual journal, *Gusts*. Here in Quebec, English-language poets can join the Black Tea Haiku Group. The French-language haiku community is particularly active: they have regular meetings in Montreal and Quebec City and a summer workshop in Baie-Comeau. Also, a number of small presses exist that publish French-language haiku and tanka – many more than we presently have in the English world.

The disadvantages of being a small community are that we are often marginalized and lack the opportunities of interaction with a larger, more diversified literary world. I am currently Books Editor of *Ribbons*, a publication of the Tanka Society of America and the largest English-language tanka journal. In the small, closely knit world of tanka, it's often difficult to be as critical and honest about poets' work as I would like. Without open and genuine feedback, it's difficult for individual poets and tanka in general to move ahead.

## Do you think that writing in English in Quebec is a political act?

Haiku and tanka are not generally political in spirit, but they can be. I write for personal reasons, but to write in English is political in the sense that it is keeping a culture alive and giving it a voice to describe that presence. I believe we need writers to define who we are and to make us aware of our world. I'm very glad that Ian Stephens, for instance, wrote about St. Henri and David Fennario writes plays about Pointe St-Charles, near where I lived for many years. But the French experience differs from ours. We need English writers to capture and explain our experience.

## Why do you write?

I write to keep myself balanced and sane, to keep myself alive and thinking, and to preserve moments otherwise ephemeral. I write for myself and others. I feel that I am able to share something important. I also love craft and developing a sense of mastery.

## Do you write with the intention of "growing a manuscript" or do you work on individual poems that are later collected into a book?

I've done both. Usually I look over what I've written, identify recurring themes,

> THE GREAT THING ABOUT HAIKU IS THAT IT CAN BE DONE ANYTIME, ANYWHERE. YOU JUST NEED TO SLIP IT INTO YOUR LIFE.

then select one and consciously explore it further.

## What is your favourite time and place to write?

It varies depending on my situation. The great thing about haiku is that it can be done anytime, anywhere. You just need to slip it into your life. But mostly it is done outside. It's not "desk" work.

## Who is your audience?

My audience includes people who love nature, who meditate or are interested in various aspects of Japanese culture, as well as artists and other poets. I am also continually surprised at the number of people I encounter who tell me they write haiku or would like to. Haiku has been called the world's most democratic poetry form: It's so short, possesses just a few simple rules, and uses such commonplace language that virtually anyone can write it – from young children (my own son started to write when he was only six years old) to seniors, and is popular as well with English Second Language students.

## Can you talk about your experience giving haiku workshops in schools?

I find kids in particular enjoy haiku and they are often my most enthusiastic audience, as well as being talented writers themselves. I usually follow the Japanese tradition of conducting an anonymous workshop: No one puts their names to the poems we discuss, so no one feels put on the spot. Everyone in the class is able to take part. More times than not, it turns out it's not the teacher's or the so-called smart kid's haiku that is voted the best in the class, but the poem by the kid no one suspected capable. I love when that happens.

## Is there an audience, outside of friends or other poets, for poetry?

Yes, but in today's intellectual climate it's difficult for people to come to poetry. For most, poetry seems inaccessible and/or irrelevant. We need to build bridges that help people get past their negative perceptions and develop an appreciation for poetry. As one example of bridge-building: For several years, I organized a haiku weekend at the Japanese Garden of the Montreal Botanical Garden. We had a book table and various haiku workshops and activities, some of which incorporated music, dance, or film. Visitors who happened to be in the garden – on a good day up to 1000! – chanced on our event and were delighted. Another instance was when my son and I spent a week at a summer camp in Quebec's Eastern Townships run by the Newman Centre of McGill. I advertised a haiku workshop on the beach for the parents, but it was the kids who came. They enjoyed it so much they requested we continue to meet. As

ANGELA LEUCK

the week went on, the parents became curious and started showing up and wrote some haiku, too. Introducing kids to poetry early is vital, and a current project of mine is a haiku anthology for teens.

## Does your day job impact on your writing?

I have tried as much as possible to be a full-time writer, and have experimented with many ways to achieve this, including part-time editing and publicity work, running a homestay business, and teaching ESL, most recently in central China. Mainly, my writing is separate from my work.

## How many drafts do you usually go through before you are satisfied with a poem?

Some come out pretty much right the first time, others can take years, and a lot never work no matter how much I revise. In the case of the following tanka, I went through a number of drafts before I reached what I consider the final version. The challenge with such short poetry forms as haiku and tanka is always to focus and distill the idea, while at the same time not being too direct. Following is a series of versions of the same poem.

> a long line
> of Canada geese heading north
> takes the shape
> of a question mark –
> your call last night

> above your house too
> a long line of Canada geese
> heading north
> takes the shape of a question mark –
> your unanswered question

> your phone call
> full of questions I have
> no answer to
> this morning a long line of Canada geese
> takes the shape of a question mark

> this evening
> when I have no answers
> a long line of Canada geese
> takes on the shape
> of a question mark

– published in *red lights*, Vol. 3, No. 2, June 2007

## What is the toughest part of writing for you?

The toughest part of writing is just keeping going. It's so easy to lose the momentum. Sometimes I can't write anything at all, but I've learned that this is a time of quiet and new ideas will come. Another challenge is believing that haiku is worthwhile. Some people say, "Well, why don't you write 'real' poetry," as if it's a matter of graduating to something bigger and better. Ironically, haiku is one of the most difficult forms of poetry to write. Basho said if you can write five good haiku, you can consider yourself a haiku poet. If you can write five great haiku, you can call yourself a haiku master. So far there are only four haiku poets that critics agree are masters. In haiku, everything has to work and be original. It's very hard to accomplish, and if you do succeed, you've still only got three lines. It's difficult in our society, which is all about output, to justify such an apparently slight form.

## What is your idea of a muse?

The concept of a muse is alien to haiku. The whole point of Zen was to get rid of everything between you and the

ANGELA LEUCK

experience. Haiku uses simple language, concrete imagery, and the present tense. Your eyes and senses are your muse; it's more a matter of getting yourself (and your inner muse) out of the way!

## Is travel important to your writing?

Seeing new places can be helpful for haiku or tanka, although it takes time to get to know a place and get beyond simple cliché. I went on a writer's retreat to Saskatchewan that was very good and travelling now to China has inspired some poems. But travel is not necessary for a haiku poet.

## Do you write about Quebec?

I write about place, which happens at the moment to be Quebec. I don't write about it because it's Quebec, but because it's where I am. I'm presently living in the Eastern Townships, where my husband and I have just bought a house. The mix of woodland, hills, and farmland has inspired Leonard Cohen, Ian Tait, Rod Willmot, and other poets who also wrote haiku. I look forward to continuing that tradition. ∎

ANGELA LEUCK

## Haiku from *Marionette on a Shelf*

marionette on a shelf –
his fingers know
how to move me

shelling peas
he thinks we could
be soul mates

his smile –
the slow smooth bend
of the river

pussywillows –
he wakes me with
a whisker rub

### Tanka

my world –
the perfect white globe
of a dandelion
that one breath from you
explodes


should I blame
it on love
or pink bougainvillea –
the kiss
by the flower vender's stall?


in front of the church
apple blossoms
like confetti
I daydream of weddings
until the hearse pulls up

# Endre Farkas

ENDRE FARKAS

**Endre Farkas was born in Hungary. His family escaped during the 1956 Hungarian uprising and settled in Montreal. He has published eleven books of poetry and plays. His work has been translated into French, Spanish, Italian, Slovenian and Turkish. He has read and performed widely in Canada, the U.S., Latin America, and Europe, and has created pieces that have toured across the country and abroad. In 1983, his book _How To_ was shortlisted for the A.M. Klein Award. A co-founding editor of _Poetry Quebec_, he is the two-time regional winner of the CBC Poetry "Face Off" Competition. His play, _Haunted House_, based on the life and work of the poet A.M. Klein, was produced in Montreal in February 2009.**

**In 2012, his collaborative book and videopoem _Blood is Blood_ was a winner of Zebra's International Poetry Film Festival in Berlin.**

_Poetry Quebec:_ **Tell us about your roots.**

_Endre Farkas:_ I was born in Hungary. My parents fled during the 1956 uprising because in my village the cry of the revolutionary mob was "Kill the Commies! Kill the Jews." My parents, Holocaust survivors, didn't need to be told twice. We escaped just as the Russians were crushing the uprising. I have lived in and around Montreal ever since.

**When did you first become interested in poetry?**

Hungary is the land of poetry and poets. At least it was when I lived there. My mother once said that even the butchers of Hungary – she wasn't only referring to literal butchers – recited poetry. It even has a national poem (the National Song) by Petöfi Sandor. Students started memorizing poems in grade 1. I still remember parts of "Lullaby" by Josef Attila that I had to know by heart. However, I only became (seriously) interested in writing poetry after a friend in high school introduced me to the Beats, especially Gregory Corso and Allen Ginsberg. I liked their "yawping."

**How did you encounter your first Quebec poem?**

Probably the first Quebec poet that I paid real attention to was A.M. Klein.

He had gone to the same high school as me (Baron Byng, also the Alma Mater of Layton and Richler), was a child of immigrants who had fled a pogrom, and wrote about living in my neighbourhood. But as a child of the '60s, it was Cohen who first really made a lasting impression on me. He wrote in what I thought was the poetic voice...the melancholic dark lyrical mystical voice.

## Why do you write?

I don't know why I started to write. Maybe because English wasn't my first language so writing seemed an adventure to understand the origins of words and how best to use them. My mother loves poetry and still occasionally quotes lines to me. I also write because I have no choice. Through writing, I better understand the world that is – and myself. In a sense I write, therefore the world is – and I am.

## What is your working definition of a poem?

A poem, more than other written art forms, is about the awareness of language. When I get the feeling that no other word, combination of words, line breaks, stanza breaks, etc., will do, then I get a feeling and an awareness that I am in the presence of a poem.

## Do you have a writing ritual?

I used to have one but now I don't. I used to like writing late at night. I thought that it was the time for poetry. I believed that strange things happened under the cloak of night. Writing poems was one of them. But now, I believe that strange things go on 24/7, including the writing of poems. I used to like smoking cigarettes, usually after I felt that I had written a good line or two. It would be like a stanza break. I would light up, read the lines out loud and listen to how it sounded, take a deep breath and exhale hoping good lines would come with it. I think smoking was part of the romantic image I had of a poet. In one of my poems, "What you should know to be a Poet" (actually a collaborative piece with Gary Snyder's poem from which I took the title), I respond to his admonition to know "your own six senses, with a watchful elegant mind" with "I have stopped smoking cigarettes/find myself susceptible to colds//my taste buds are in bloom again./Makes it difficult to drink the water//though I still can't cut a straight line/I still intend to build a home//even now/I feel my lines breathe cleaner."

## Who is your favourite Quebec poet?

A.M. Klein and artie gold. I think Klein was Canada's first urban poet. He was the first Canadian poet to map a Canadian city (Montreal) poetically, see its topographic, cultural, linguistic, political and sacred geography. He wrote about his cultural heritage in a regional and cosmopolitan manner. He experimented with language, mixing French, English and Yiddish. He wrote sympathetically of the "French canadien" unlike the spoofing Dr. Drummond.

artie gold was the first true Canadian "hipster." He was also a city poet. He shot the city into his veins and it flowed from his pen. His first book, *cityflowers,* is a wonderful ode to living here. I also was and continue to be in awe of the way he makes jumps and connections. I also like Jean-Paul Daoust. My reading of French is limited but his "urbanity" and performance/readings are engaging and lively and provocative.

ENDRE FARKAS

## Do you think that writing in English in Quebec is a political act?

Yes, I think it is. It is because the Quebec nationalists make it so. Quebec has a language bill that makes it so. It exempts the written arts from the rules and regulations of Bill 101 but that very exemption makes it political. It implies that writing poems, stories and plays are *allowed* by the grace and magnanimity of the majority. I am allowed to write in English. Most English language writers in Quebec aren't conscious of this reality. I am. Maybe it's because of my parents' history and what they went through because of right-wing nationalism and then living under occupation of a foreign power (Russia) and because of friends who have lived under dictatorships that I am more sensitive to it.

## What is your approach to writing a poem: inspiration-driven, structural, social, thematic... ?

All of the above. Sometimes (rarely) it comes in one fell swoop from what might be called inspiration, the mystical phone call that comes at the oddest and rarest of times. Sometimes out of that mystical message comes the structural. *Murders in the Welcome Café* is an example of that. One night, walking through Chinatown, I passed the Welcome Café and had a "déjà-vu" that murders had been committed there. Out of that momentary infinitesimal lag in the operation of two co-active sensory nerve centres that commonly function simultaneously – two years later – came a thirteen-poem series that became a hardboiled detective chapbook. The social/political poems come from a reaction to a realpolitik issue. Most of the time a poem comes from me showing up,

sitting down and working and discovering what I need to write.

## Do you write about Quebec?

I think Quebec is not only a place but a state of mind and all that that implies. It is a condition and it's about language. And perhaps because of that I am more aware of the "mot juste" in a poem. My Quebec tends to be Montreal, a city that has been inspiration to both English and French. It's a city-state that is vibrant, a pain in the ass, an addiction and a lover. Yes. Oui. I write "out of" Québec/Kwee-bek. How can I not? I live here. Je me souviens.

## Do you think that being part of the English-speaking minority in Quebec influences what or how you write?

Having come of poetic age during the turbulent times of the '70s and '80s in Quebec, having friends who were ardent nationalists, I could not but be affected. I knew I was writing in the language of the "oppressor." Even though I knew being an immigrant and coming of age in the '60s had very little to do with being the oppressor – having experienced being oppressed – I had sympathies for their aspirations. However, not being a *pure laine*, I was told I was one of "les autres." Also having gone through the English school system, I could not help feeling that I was on the wrong side. When I ran the Véhicule reading series with artie gold, I approached a francophone poet about doing bilingual readings. I was told that it was politically impossible for them to participate in such a project with "us."

I was conscious of the situation and wrote about it, wrote out of it. In my collection, *Face Off,* I have a poem (Habs 6,

ENDRE FARKAS

Bruins 1) about the conflict: "Dryden vs Larocque/we used to argue about percentages/ but now/ accents." However, it was in the poetry performance piece *Face off/Mise au Jeu* that I explored the language/cultural debate. It was a commissioned piece by a dance company which had English, French. American, Jewish, Protestant and Catholic (lapsed) members. It was during the time of the 1980 referendum that the piece was performed. It was bilingual and dealt with the conflict on personal, cultural and political levels. I have also written other poems that deal with this theme, most of the time in a satiric vein: "Love in Quebec" and "Language Cops" are two examples. I have also incorporated French phrases into some my poems, not because it is politically correct but because they were the right words/"les mots juste."

**How has taking poetry from the page to the stage infused or energized your writing? Do you think performance poetry or multidisciplinary poetry impacts readership? Has it increased your own audience?**

I've always thought that poetry readings are performances. This may be because of having seen poets like Ginsberg, bill bissett and the Four Horsemen perform in my early poetic life. Maybe also because of the many boring readings that I attended and because of my affiliation with Véhicule Art gallery where I was introduced to performance art. While hanging out at the gallery, I also encountered artists from different disciplines who were interested in collaborating. These collaborations led me to create pieces that were conceived specifically for performance. These were not "page" poems but performance poems. They were structured differently. They took into consideration time, space and movement. The form tended to be modular and minimal in text. i.e. a poem entitled "As the breath is the journey, I move and it is imperceptible as is the breath just breathed in and out" is also the entire poem. This piece was created for dancers and played on and with the images and concept of breath and movement. It is also a sound poem with each word being breathed, sounded, stretched and modulated. This poem doesn't work on the page and most page-limited readers would not, could not, relate to it unless they attended a performance. And of course, most don't. I don't know if it has increased my audience but I know I have presented to a diversified audience, which I like.

**For the past forty years, beginning with your time as a Vehicle poet, you have been a key figure on the Montreal scene, having worked hard to bridge the divide between poetry and the public. Among other things, you were a founding editor of Véhicule Press, you founded The Muses' Company, you curated the *Circus of Words*, you put poems on Montreal buses, and you were a co-founder of *Poetry Quebec*. What has been the motivation behind all these efforts?**

I didn't consciously start out to do all these things. They came along because I met certain people at certain times in certain situations. Doing these things seemed to be the right thing to do at the time and it was "fun." Partly because

> A POEM IS AN ORGANIC AND LIVING ENTITY. AND, AS HUMANS CHANGE OVER TIME, I THINK A POEM MAY AS WELL.

the English-language poetry scene in Montreal was in the doldrums in the late '60s and early '70s and it was a way for me to get my own work and that of others – friends – out there, I did it. It didn't seem so hard. And one thing led to another, and because I was doing it, I gained a cultural, social and political awareness of the implications of what I was doing and with it, a certain expertise. And, of course, most of this was done collectively or collaboratively. My essay, "Confessions of a Collaborator" in *Vehicule Days* (Signature Editions) goes into it in more detail.

**Who is your audience?**

First, it's me. Then, the "audience of one" (the other), the ideal reader who isn't me. The reader who appreciates the work that went into it. Then the millions who are eagerly waiting to read it. And, finally, those who are yet to be born.

**Do you think there is an audience, outside of friends or other poets, for poetry?**

If I am brutally honest, then I have to admit that there is no audience for poetry. When I am less brutal, I admit that there is a small audience. But the real question is why do we (humans) write poems /make art? In the Darwinian sense, creatures do what they do primarily to survive and propagate the species. They adapt to do that, they grow bigger/ shorter wings, sharper claws, thicker fur, etc. One of the appendages that

humans evolved is their creativity. The writing of poems is one form of this. So it's not about audience, it's about survival of the species. Also having edited *PQ* and seeing 300 to 500 people online at any one time, makes me think that there is an audience.

**Having seen these numbers, which seem almost unbelievable, what is your view of publishing digitally? Would you consider publishing your next collection as an e-book? And given the choice between publishing online, and getting the numbers, or publishing fewer than a thousand paper copies, which would you pick?**

I don't think it's one or the other, though given the reality of fewer presses doing fewer books, more and more poets seeking part of that shrinking pie, longer and longer wait times to see a book move from acceptance to publication, fewer and fewer independent bookstores that *might* carry the books, fewer and fewer newspapers reviewing poetry books, distribution costs, and lack of promotion opportunities, e-books seem like a solution. And the audience potential on the net is much greater. It's global.

There are, of course, all the objections and problems that come with e-publishing – from the vanity publishing smear to no editorial quality control.

And, of course, the absence of the arti-fact (the book).

**How does your day job impact on your writing?**

When I did have one teaching, it gave me the financial security and freedom to give myself over to the arts, to writing. It also allowed me to be in the company of other people who believed that poetry was important. I was fortunate to have such a day job. It also made me feel that I had the responsibility to write because it was not only a private, self-indulgent act but a public, social and political re-sponsibility. This sounds pompous and self-aggrandizing but again the writers (from dictatorships) I associated with made me realize the importance of the role of the writer as a loudmouth witness.

**Which poem or poems of yours have made the most noise, or put you in the position of having to take a stand that might have been dangerous or unpopular? Has any of your writing ever gotten you into trouble?**

Life-threatening? None. No Fatwa yet, although my most recent one, the two-voice videopoem *Blood is Blood* (with Carolyn Marie Souaid) has stirred the most discussion and polarization. It is a poetic dialogue between Jew and Arab. We have had people walk out during performances; accuse us of na-ivety and even-handedness. We've also had requests to modify – censor – it for performance.

**How many drafts do you usually go through before you are satis-fied with a poem?**

I've been accused of over-editing, over-revising. I may revise only five or six times but it may be over a three- or four-year period. My rhythm has been a man-uscript/book every four or five years. I am also not averse to changing a poem even if it has been published. Just because it is published doesn't mean that it's set in stone. A poem is an organic and living entity. And, as humans change over time, I think a poem may as well.

**Do you write with the intention of "growing a manuscript" or do you work on individual poems that are later collected into a book?**

Right from the start, I "grew manuscripts." It wasn't a conscious decision. My first book *Szerbusz* grew out of a return visit to Hungary. I just wrote poems while there, and when I came back I saw that there was an arc. The arc was both through the topics and the form. I noticed that there was a strong use of repetition. This has stuck with me over the years and I have used it in various ways. Although poems are individual entities, as they accumu-late, I begin to see a thread of a thematic or structural narrative. Once I begin to see that, which sometimes happens ear-ly on, other times much later, I become schizophrenic in seeing the poem as a poem on its own and seeing the poem in the grand scheme of a manuscript.

**What is the toughest part of writ-ing for you?**

The start. The blank paper. The middle, finding it. The end. Hearing the "that's it!" However, on the whole, I haven't really had what is called "writer's block." On the whole, I've found writing a pleasur-able pain.

**Do you have a favourite time and place to write?**

As I mentioned earlier, I used to like writing at night. I still do but no longer only then. As to place, when I am away I like to sit in a café and write longhand (what a strange expression). At home, I keyboard peck.

## Is travel important to your writing?

I don't like to travel. I like being in different places but not the getting there, especially if it means flying. Being in different places is good because it dislocates me. This dislocation also dislocates my writing. I write differently. I am more disciplined than when at home. I keep a journal and write by hand. I've been doing a series "Proemcards from..." One series that has been published is *Proemcards from Chile*. It's my postcards to friends and myself. I don't know too many people who send postcards anymore. I also think of them as my snapshots which I retouch once home.

## What is your idea of a muse?

Life. Death. Everything in between. ∎

Sometimes a first or early version is an assemblage of life's fragments, of odds — and I do mean odds — and ends of sounds, images, and phrases. Later versions are attempts to give it coherence and shape, if not meaning. — EF

## Fragments

Good news is always a postponement.
There is a bookshelf
up against the wall
legs spread being frisked
about to be cuffed

eine kleine nachtmusic
a hip hop lullaby rocking the cradle
and sleep slips undercover
next to the sniper

sliced to the bone
words meatless

no time for language
so settle for silent lungs
grateful for a smokeless Saturday
it's in the eyes that would say something

name, sense, numb across the heaving chest
and blindness is
postponed by stronger phrases

## Fragments

Good news is always a postponement
A temporary shelter

There is a bookshelf I like
Up against the wall

Eine kleine nacht music
Hip hop lullabye rocking the crib

Sleep is a sniper
The goodnight kiss of an obsession

Sliced to the bones
Words meatless

Grateful for a smokeless Saturday
The eyes that would say something

The senses heave across the chest
Curled into news

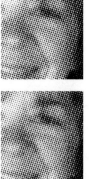

# Carolyn Marie Souaid

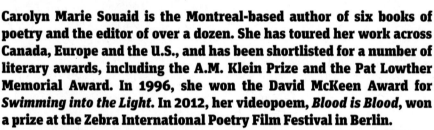

**Carolyn Marie Souaid is the Montreal-based author of six books of poetry and the editor of over a dozen. She has toured her work across Canada, Europe and the U.S., and has been shortlisted for a number of literary awards, including the A.M. Klein Prize and the Pat Lowther Memorial Award. In 1996, she won the David McKeen Award for *Swimming into the Light*. In 2012, her videopoem, *Blood is Blood*, won a prize at the Zebra International Poetry Film Festival in Berlin.**

**From 2008 to 2011, she served as poetry editor for Signature Editions, one of Canada's top publishers of poetry, and, in 2009, was one of the founding editors of *Poetry Quebec*, the first online review showcasing the English-language poetry and poets of Quebec. In 2013, she was awarded a seven-week writer's residency at the Banff Arts Centre.**

**Souaid holds an M.A. in Creative Writing from Concordia University.**

### Poetry Quebec: Where are you from?

*Carolyn Marie Souaid:* I was born in the Royal Victoria Hospital in Montreal. Both my maternal and paternal grandparents came to Canada from Lebanon in the early 1900s to make a new life for themselves. My mother was raised in Toronto, my father, in a small French-speaking town outside Montreal called St. Hyacinthe. That's also where I spent my early years, where I went to "maternelle." My young, Beatle-crazed babysitters spoke only French to me. Friday nights, they bundled me up and took me to the local greasy spoon to listen to the latest of the British Invasion on the jukebox. We moved from St. Hyacinthe to St. Lambert on the south shore of Montreal just before Expo 67, when I was six, and I remained there – except for the three years I spent teaching the Inuit of Arctic Quebec – until very recently.

### When did you encounter your first Quebec poem?

In high school. A poem set to music called "Lindberg" by Robert Charlebois. I was in the enriched stream of grade 9 French and we had a teacher who seemed intent on introducing us to some of the key figures in Québécois culture – artists like Félix Leclerc and

Gilles Vigneault. She had a little portable record player set up at the back of the classroom, and she made us listen to the song over and over again while we followed along with the words on the page. I wasn't aware of it at the time, but things were beginning to heat up in Quebec. The October Crisis was still fresh in people's minds. René Levesque was getting ready to sweep into power. Ironically, the teacher was an anglophone. I still don't understand where her motivation came from – maybe she was married to a francophone – but I'm now grateful to her for opening that door.

## What was your first introduction to poetry?

Christmas 1965. My aunt, who was also an English teacher, gave me a copy of *A Child's Garden of Verses* by Robert Louis Stevenson. It had beautiful colour illustrations. I still have the book, though the jacket's long gone. I read it cover to cover every night before bed. Three years later she took me to see Zeffirelli's *Romeo and Juliet,* which technically is also poetry, though I didn't know it at the time. She didn't seem to care that I was only eight. She felt that it was a necessary part of my education.

## You've said elsewhere that you *hated* poetry as a kid. Your previous comment seems to contradict this.

In high school, I found poetry intimidating. Back then, the teacher's approach was never "How does this poem sit with you?" but rather "What is the hidden message?" It felt more like being at the dissection table in biology class. There was a sense that if you could identify the component parts, then somehow you could determine what the poem "meant," as though there was only one possible answer. This nonsense has influenced my approach as an educator. I believe that one can enjoy a poem without fully "understanding" it, the same way that I can get enjoyment out of opera or contemporary dance without having any scholastic training in them. My incomplete knowledge may limit my experience, but it doesn't take away from my appreciation of those things on some level.

## How does this work in practical terms in the classroom?

The starting point should always be the *affective* response to a poem. Does it touch or move you? Do you like it? What don't you like about it? And so on. Once students can identify how they feel about a poem, we can start to examine the techniques used to achieve the end result. Back when I was in high school, teachers always put us in the uncomfortable position of having to deconstruct the poem before ever responding to it on an emotional level. The worst offender of this was the high school English exam, which always included an unfamiliar poem and a barrage of technical questions about theme, personification, metaphor, etc. For my part, I always panicked. I could never seem to get a handle on it. That said, I sense that today's more student-friendly approach underemphasizes the teaching of the poetic toolkit. Some of it has to do with the generalized dumbing down of the curriculum in public school to accommodate the Twitter generation, but I think another reason is that teachers themselves are still uncomfortable teaching poetry.

## What lured you back to poetry?

I had a no-nonsense English teacher in my first year at Marianopolis College. One day she brought in "The Red Wheelbarrow" by William Carlos Williams and let us "go at it" as a group, no holds barred. I think we spent two whole classes on it, and I was awestruck that something with so few brushstrokes could provoke such rich discussion. Years later, for practical reasons, I chose to write a book of poetry as my M.A. thesis.

**Practical reasons?**

Crazy chore-filled days with a newborn, brief stretches of night in between feedings – this was my life at the time. It seemed that poetry, shorter than prose, was a form I could focus on. The short intervals of "free" time gave me the opportunity to see something to completion.

**What is your working definition of a poem?**

A poem is more than the sum total of the poet's knowledge; it's the by-product of his or her state of mind at the time of writing, which is a jumble of all experience, real or felt or imagined. The poem is a document of the poet's inner landscape, if you will. Montreal poet Robert Melançon says that for him poetry is closer to a drawing than to a novel, and I would agree with that. I also like Leonard Cohen's "If your life is burning well, poetry is just the ash." But there is a complexity to that ash. Because of its brevity and concision, poetry is the most difficult form to write and appreciate. While prose has its challenges, the demands of a poem are more rigorous, both in the reading and writing of it.

I spend a lot of time talking to students about what differentiates the two genres. Over the years, I've developed a way to talk about it that uses a simple analogy based on the "shrinking" canvases of art. I compare the novel to the sprawling floor-to-ceiling oil painting you would find in a museum. Such canvases are vast in terms of the space they cover, in the same way that a novel is a sweeping story that involves numerous characters and a proliferation of subplots. A short story is akin to something that might fit onto half a wall in a museum. With the space reined in, there is less room for the artist to spread his paint. Similarly, a short story writer has fewer pages – far less space in which to build a particular universe. The poem? It's a very small painting on the wall. Maybe there is only one thing drawing your eye in – a lone autumn tree, for instance, or a broken bicycle. But that bike is yawping precision and compression. It touches you on a most profound level.

**Do you have a writing ritual?**

Most weekdays during the school year, I work as a teacher on call. As it turns out, this sort of job offers the best payout for the least amount of effort. No take-home work at the end of the day. No meetings, minimal stress. It also leaves Saturday and Sunday, as well as the summer months, open for the possibility of writing. But at the same time it sets up a kind of write-on-demand scenario that doesn't really fit with my idea of being a writer. On "teaching" days, once the students are at work on the assigned task, I allow myself to dip into a book of poetry, or drift off into space. If the stars are aligned, an idea for a poem emerges. It isn't the most ideal of circumstances, but I take advantage of the lull, scribbling fast and furiously, or taking notes for later. When I get home, I hit the computer and occasionally I can write straight through until three o'clock in the morning without even realizing how long I've been at it. This is my ritual: squeezing in time whenever I can. When I'm "in the zone" – that is to say, when I'm having a productive week – the ideas start coming at the most inopportune times. Like while I'm in the shower. Or driving. I've been known to get the bones of a poem down in the time it takes for a red light to turn green. When the risk for an accident is high, I pull over to the side of the road. Another writing environment that works for me is the café. Some of my best ideas find their way onto restaurant napkins. I love sitting with a strong cup of black coffee, a ballpoint pen, and a clean white napkin.

**Do you write with the intention of "growing a manuscript" or do you work on individual poems that are later collected into a book?**

I always work with the idea of growing a manuscript. But I don't start off right away knowing what that manuscript is going to be. I just write poems. At a certain point I figure out what state of mind I am in, what my preoccupations are, why I am writing a particular kind of poem. Once I have a sense of that, a manuscript starts to take shape. It seems that one poem can't capture all I want to say about something. I see each of my books as a multi-faceted investigation into whatever my obsession is at that time, each poem being a single note in the composition, a morsel of the broader inquiry.

**Specifically, how do you approach the writing of a poem?**

I don't have one approach. It depends on my frame of mind at the time of the writing. And on the voracity of my concentration.

**What do you mean by that?**

In an interview with *The Paris Review*, Ted Hughes recalled a time when he earned a living as a teacher in England. He said the experience taught him "the terrific exhaustion of that profession." Said he wanted to "keep his energy for himself" as if he "had the right." This has stuck with me, and is part of the reason why I have never, except for three years in my twenties, and once when I needed the cash, taught full-time. If you're dedicated, it's just too demanding. It drains me of the creative energy I need to write. I am now discovering that even some of the freelance writing work I take saps my energy, and I am slowly trying to free myself from these contractual obligations.

**When the creative drive is present, which approach is closest to the way you work?**

It varies. The difficulty of truly connecting with the "Other" has been a recurring theme in my work. *Swimming into the Light*, my first collection, was the starting point of an ongoing inquiry into the unbridgeable chasm that exists between people. My focus in this case was adoption. I wondered whether the bond between an adoptive mother and her adopted child would be different from the one between a biological mother and her natural child. My next book, *October*, examined the physical and emotional distance between the "two solitudes" in Quebec. *Snow Formations* explored the intersecting and contradictory worlds of natives and non-natives – mainly whites – along the Hudson-Ungava coast of Northern Quebec.

CAROLYN MARIE SOUAID

These early books were also driven by the need to be a faithful witness to my time and place, as Mordecai Richler used to say. They dealt with the social and cultural issues of my immediate surroundings. I'm thinking, in particular, of collections such as *Satie's Sad Piano*, set in the aftermath of Pierre Trudeau's death, and again, *October*, focusing on the October Crisis of 1970. In each of these books, I made a conscious decision to depict a particular socio-cultural moment in Quebec, although *Satie's Sad Piano* was more of an experiment in voice and form.

*Blood is Blood*, a collaboration with Endre Farkas, was fuelled by the July War in 2006, a 34-day military conflict in Lebanon and northern Israel between Hezbollah paramilitary forces and the Israeli military. The personal e-mails between us in response to the conflict morphed into a two-voice piece, then an audio poem, and finally a book-length poem and video. In this case, politics triggered the creative act and, of course, the emotional reactions in each of us: Endre a child of Holocaust survivors and me, of Lebanese-Christian ancestry whose "homeland" was again under attack. But the book was yet another inquiry into the gulf that separates people.

While I was writing *Paper Oranges*, the structures in my personal life were crumbling, and this significantly altered my process. The poems in it are less accessible, more playful. I was more interested in experimenting with the musicality of words, less in imposing a narrative arc on the book. Ultimately, *Paper Oranges* is a mood piece.

**How do your Quebec-focused books document your "time and place"?**

Just to backtrack for a little context: I developed an interest in the long poem while taking a graduate class with Gary Geddes at Concordia University in 1991. That year, we looked at a variety of writers including Daphne Marlatt, Dionne Brand, Christopher Dewdney, Roy Kiyooka, bp-Nichol and others. I liked the expansive canvas of the long poem, which I equated to the novel, and this influenced the form of my first three collections. If you read the poems in those books, in order, there is something of a beginning, middle, and end. There are characters. There is setting, conflict, and resolution. But my long poem comes closer to an abstract work than a representational one in that the reader also bears some responsibility in making meaning.

My three "Quebec-focused" books are all structured very differently, however. *October* was written as a more conventional narrative. It has that feel of a novel I was talking about. As you progress through it, you meet the characters; you get their stories. The first half of the book looks at Quebec's infamous October Crisis through the eyes of a ten-year-old; the second half examines the workings of a linguistically mixed marriage. In the broader context, this couple is also a microcosm of Canada, built primarily on the two founding cultures, English and French. It is a story I had to tell, having been raised in Quebec, and having experienced first-hand the fallout from the politically turbulent times: In 1970, St. Lambert was suddenly thrown into the spotlight because "terrorists" kidnapped Quebec's Labour Minister, Pierre Laporte. It happened three kilometres from my house. He had been playing ball with his son when a car slowed

CAROLYN MARIE SOUAID

down and yanked him off the street in plain view. A state of apprehended insurrection was declared and the War Measures Act came down, suspending civil liberties and personal freedoms. Helicopters flew over our schools. The army tanks rolled. Panic reigned over our sleepy little town.

Quebec, but more specifically Montreal, figures prominently in *Satie's Sad Piano*. Written in the spirit of George Elliott Clarke's *Whylah Falls* and Michael Ondaatje's *Collected Works of Billy the Kidd*, it features a cast of eclectic characters or "voices" who bear witness to the Trudeaumania of the late '60s. Written as a multi-voiced stream of consciousness, it is my most experimental and least accessible work. None of the poems are titled. The so-called characters with speaking parts include Mont-Royal, Radio, and Pierre Trudeau, in absentia. Interestingly, not long after my book was published, and after reviewing it favourably, George Elliott Clarke came out with his Trudeau opera. (I'm just saying.)

The third of my "Quebec" books is *Snow Formations*, which focuses on a very narrow subset of the province and looks at the ways that cultures inevitably leave their imprint on one another, the good and the bad. The book consists of several poem-pairings, such as "Still Life" and "Still, Life" and "Teacher Gives Hazy Account" and "The Student" that reverberate and play off each other, forcing readers to re-evaluate their own received truths about the world.

**Does being part of the English-speaking minority in Quebec influence your writing?**

It was definitely the impetus for *October*. Married at the time to a francophone

with nationalist politics, the book was an effort to try to reconcile the warring factions in Quebec. I believed, rather naively at the time, that it was possible for opposites with some affinity to one another to experience a true connection, with compassion and understanding. So I wrote toward that eventuality. The last poem in *October,* written in French, was a symbolic gesture on my part, a genuine effort to make peace.

**Do you feel you were successful?**

All during the revision process I kept telling Michael Harris, my editor, that it wasn't working, the poems weren't bringing the solitudes together. If anything, there was too much keeping them apart. The material wasn't there. To which he replied, "Maybe it's an impossibility." I would say that the book was a successful failure.

**Do you think that writing in English in Quebec is a political act?**

Everything we do in Quebec is political. Everything. It's the nature of living here. But writing in English for me is probably less political than going into a grocery store and addressing the cashier in English, which I have started to do more often these days, and without remorse, because the writing I do is private, and English is my mother tongue. It's as natural for me to write my poems in English, as it is to chew gum or go for a walk. Few francophones are exposed to my English on the page, where it lies silently. On the other hand, deliberately speaking English in public in Quebec – now that's making a statement. Especially when, like me, you are fluently bilingual. It says, loud and clear, *I live here too!* I am every much as "Québécois" as you. It's a political act I feel I must make to ensure that anglophones, who have made significant contributions to Quebec history, continue receiving services in English. I, of course, can do this because I speak the language of the majority. My action carries more weight because it doesn't come from a place of intolerance and narrow-mindedness. I'm not a unilingual anglophone who's been here all her life and can't speak of word of French.

## Why do you write?

I write because it would be impossible for me to live and not write. Writing makes my life coherent. The other reasons are (a) I like to share what is unique about myself yet what is common to others; (b) I like the problem-solving component involved in mapping the subtle, surprising, or previously unrecognized connections between things.

## Who is your audience?

I write the poem to please myself. If it doesn't please me, it probably won't please a reader. So I work on it until it does. Sometimes it takes many drafts, and many days or weeks, or even months. It can take years. Occasionally I work on it too long and I kill it. But I'm ruthless. When it's dead, it's dead. If I can't bring it back, I scrap it altogether. I hate keeping dribs and drabs of half-assed writing in my files.

## Do you think there is an audience, outside of friends or other poets, for poetry?

Definitely. But I think that audience is still in its infancy. I'm thinking of people who hark back to poetry when they need a profound quote for a wedding toast or eulogy, or when they want to sound "cultured" at a cocktail party. That audience understands that there is something in poetry that can "say the unsayable." This is a good start, but poets still have a lot of work to do to expand those numbers and, more importantly, stoke the fire: to make them want to read poetry because they want to read poetry. No other reason. The single biggest hindrance to opening poetry up to a wider readership are the Ivory Tower poets who write Ivory Tower poems to give Ivory Tower academics material to write about, those more interested in securing themselves a place in the literary pantheon than in moving a reader.

**Writing is a solitary activity in which you spend a lot of time with yourself, within yourself. This can lead to insecurity and doubt about yourself and your work. Do you experience this and if so, how do you deal with it?**

Frankly, I like being alone with my writing. It's the best part of being a writer – playing with the puzzle until you make something you're happy with. What's hard is getting shortlisted for a literary award and then being passed over. Intellectually, I know that juries are subjective. I've sat on them. Change the jury and a different winner emerges. But it doesn't take away from the feelings of rejection when *your* book isn't the one selected. It's such a roller coaster. One minute you're up, the next you're down. Last year, after *Blood is Blood* won at the Zebra International Poetry Film Festival in Berlin, it buoyed my confidence. Prizes shouldn't have such an effect, but of course, they do.

## How important is recognition for you? What does it mean?

Any writer who says that it doesn't matter would be lying. Otherwise, why publish? Why not just scratch away in the dark, and then light a match to it? The problem is that there are so many writers fighting for a piece of the pie – whether it's a book review or a literary prize. And the pie isn't that big. So many out there never get their due. And if you measure your worth by that yardstick – and it's hard not to – it can be disheartening. I am lucky in that my books have been widely reviewed and have made several shortlists over the years. I don't know whether or not this translates into book sales, but it has certainly made me feel that what I am doing is appreciated by a segment of the population that matters to me.

## What is the toughest part of writing for you?

Getting started. If I have a "free" day – a day I don't have to teach – circumstances dictate that I have ample time to roll up my sleeves and get the bones of something down on paper. But it doesn't always work that way for me. It's easier to notice all the housework that has piled up, the dust balls, the overflowing laundry in the hamper. I am fairly disorganized. As I said, ideas come when I should be concentrating on something else, like a conversation I'm having with someone who matters.

## What is your idea of a muse?

Some of my past muses have been real people. But now, my muse is usually another poem or book of poems that fires me up enough to want to write a poem myself.

## Is travel important to your writing?

Unfortunately, my home office is too connected to my everyday world of work. It doesn't stimulate my imagination. Travel is important insofar as it takes me out of my quotidian experience. I find my best writing happens when I am away – walking along the beach or wandering unfamiliar streets in Europe. A particular beach town in Maine has always been a source of inspiration for me. The rhythm of the waves centres me enough to free my mind. Being elsewhere knocks me off balance and lets me see the world through a different lens. Ironically, that "other" place opens up the channels so I can write about home in a fresh way. ∎

CAROLYN MARIE SOUAID

*Two Incarnations of the Same Poem*

### Throat Song

It was the end of God and abstractions, my last year
in school. Dusk penetrating a shingle
beach house. The suffocating
humidity.

Bedside, a few thin volumes. Beckett and
his dark oeuvre.

       Who knows how it happened, or why –
a mysterious bird arrived on my sill
like so much light,

puffing up his chest,

the raspberry sky
speaking mountains
through him.

Shifting my attention to the salted particulars:
algae, starfish,
the ordinary
granular sea
out there.

Making the wait /
weight bearable.

## Throat Song (Refrain)

Darkness. A tree. Dry grass husks.

Until.

Who knows how it happened, or why –
a goldfinch arrived like so much
light, puffing up his chest,

the raspberry sky
speaking mountains
through him.

And the miracle wasn't plankton
or the white tulle flounce of sea,
it wasn't God
clothed in the everyday breath of earth,

the miracle was the weight
itself, suddenly bearable.

# Acknowledgements

**Mark Abley** • "Labrador," by Mark Abley, in *Queen's Quarterly*, Fall 2012. "White on White," by Mark Abley, in *The New Canon: An Anthology of Canadian Poetry*, ed. Carmine Starnino, Véhicule, 2005. Reprinted in *The Silver Palace Restaurant*, McGill-Queen's University Press, 2005.

**Maxianne Berger** • "What Bleeds in August, Still," by Maxianne Berger, in *After The Mountain: The A.M. Klein Reboot Project*, ed. Jason Camlot, Synapse Press, 2011. "one red aster," by Maxianne Berger, in *Frogpond* 35:1 (winter, 2012): 16.

**Stephanie Bolster** • "25 April 1856," by Stephanie Bolster in *The Capilano Review* Series 2, No. 12. Winter 1994. "Aperture, 1856," in *White Stone: The Alice Poems* by Stephanie Bolster, Signal Editions / Véhicule Press, April 1998.

**Jason Camlot** • "Bewildered Alexandrines," from *Attention All Typewriters* by Jason Camlot, DC Books, 2005. "The Spade," from *The Debaucher* by Jason Camlot, Insomniac Press, 2008.

**Brian Campbell** • "The Stillness Minnow," from *Passenger Flight* by Brian Campbell, Signature Editions, 2009. "Mountain," by Brian Campbell, from *After The Mountain: The A.M. Klein Reboot Project*, ed. Jason Camlot, Synapse Press, 2011.

**Moe Clark** • "Twist Tobacco," by Moe Clark; from *Hearts Beating* by the Honouring Women Zine Project. Released February 14, 2013.

**Mary di Michele** • "The Blue Bowing of Evening," an unpublished poem from a current manuscript, *Bicycle Thieves*, by Mary di Michele. "Invitation to Read Wang Wei in a Montréal Snowstorm," from *Debriefing the Rose* by Mary di Michele, House of Anansi, 1998.

**Endre Farkas** • "Fragments," an unpublished poem, October 19, 2002. © Endre Farkas. "Fragments," an unpublished poem, October 23, 2002. © Endre Farkas.

**Gabe Foreman** • "Break on through," an unpublished poem, which aired on CBC Radio's *Daybreak* in May 2012. © Gabe Foreman. "Socialites," an unpublished poem. © Gabe Foreman.

**Susan Gillis** • "The Body Runs Itself but Not on Air Alone," an unpublished draft. © Susan Gillis. "Spring Storm," from *The Rapids* by Susan Gillis, Brick Books, 2012.

**Charlotte Hussey** • "Four Corners," from *Glossing the Spoils* by Charlotte Hussey, Stroud, Glos: Awen Publications, 2012.

**kaie kellough** • "échos," from *maple leaf rag* by kaie kellough, Arbeiter Ring Publishing, 2010. Written to commemorate the police shooting of a youth, Fredy Villanueva, in Montreal North in 2008.

**Catherine Kidd** • "Hyena Subpoena." First published as a text excerpt with audio in Branch: *Branch magazine*, ed. Gillian Sze and Roberutsu. Issue 5, *Wild*. Poem: *Hyena subpoena*. Branchmagazine.com, 2011.

**Angela Leuck** • Haiku by Angela Leuck, from *Marionette on a Shelf*. Haiku Canada Sheet, 2010. Tanka by Angela Leuck, from *a cicada in the cosmos*. inkling, 2010.

**Steve Luxton** • "My Late Father's Shirts" (original). Unpublished. © Steve Luxton. "My Late Father's Shirts" (revised). Unpublished. © Steve Luxton.

**David McGimpsey** • "I would never go there myself because I have the internet but I hear that Montreal's Botanical Gardens is a really great place to visit!" Unpublished. © David McGimpsey. "Starbucks makes great coffee, internet treachery, so I'm not going to pretend there's a poem which compares to pie graphs because, after all, the last review of my writing commented mostly (and negatively) about my weight." Unpublished. © David McGimpsey.

**Erín Moure** • "The Bread Truck." Unpublished. © Erín Moure. "The Martin Sequence," from *A Play in Shouts and Paraphernalia*. Unpublished. © Erín Moure.

**Robyn Sarah** • "The Orchestre du Conservatoire Rehearses in Salle St-Sulpice," from *A Day's Grace* (2003) by Robyn Sarah; reprinted with permission of the poet and The Porcupine's Quill. "Rue Jeanne Mance," from *Questions About The Stars* by Robyn Sarah (Brick Books, 1998); reprinted with permission of the poet.

**Richard Sommer** • "razor blades," from *The Other Side of Games* by Richard Sommer, Delta Canada, 1977. "Postscript." Composed in December 2011 by Richard Sommer a few weeks before his death; read by Vicki Tansey on CBC Radio, March 2012.

**Carolyn Marie Souaid** • "Throat Song," from *Snow Formations* by Carolyn Marie Souaid, Signature Editions, 2002. "Throat Song (Refrain)," from *Paper Oranges* by Carolyn Marie Souaid, Signature Editions, 2008.

**Gillian Sze** • "To John Lyman and the Portrait of his Father," excerpted from *Fish Bones* by Gillian Sze, DC Books, 2009. "Lunacy," from *Fish Bones* by Gillian Sze, DC Books, 2009. "Roses," from *The Anatomy of Clay* by Gillian Sze, ECW Press, 2011.

**Mahamud Siad Togane** • "That Time of Year," by Mahamud Togane; published in *Poetry Quebec*, Issue #5.